Culture, Celebrity, and the Cemetery

Monuments and memorials commemorating the dead and past events around the world have recently gained importance, not least because we are living in an era in which many are driven to record and archive the events of their lives. Cemeteries, in particular, are increasingly viewed as places associated with popular culture and cultural memory, with many now being considered as heritage tourism sites. *Culture, Celebrity, and the Cemetery* analyses the famous Hollywood Forever Cemetery in Los Angeles, USA, examining how the cemetery presents itself as an attraction, whilst also safeguarding and promoting cultural heritage.

Focusing on an analysis of the articulation and performance of commemoration, Levitt examines how the cemetery leverages its rich resources to draw visitors and the diverse ways in which visitors interact with the cemetery, considering the influence of celebrity culture, fandoms, and cinema culture. Combining ethnographic research with cultural analysis, the book situates Hollywood Forever in the context of cemetery development in the United States and argues that touristic visits to cemeteries more generally have become similar to visits to more traditional memorials. Providing more than just a critical analysis of this fascinating cemetery as a landscape of famous death, Levitt coherently weaves the theme of cultural memory and meaning-making throughout every chapter.

Offering the first book-length study of the cultural impact of Hollywood Forever in particular, and the cemetery as public heritage space in general, *Culture, Celebrity, and the Cemetery* will be of interest to scholars and students of heritage studies and tourism around the world.

Linda Levitt is Associate Professor of Communication Studies at Stephen F. Austin State University, USA. Her research is focused at the intersection of cultural memory and media studies.

Heritage, Tourism, and Community
Series Editors: Helaine Silverman and Mike Robinson

Heritage, Tourism, and Community is an innovative book series that seeks to address these three interconnected areas from multidisciplinary and interdisciplinary perspectives. Titles in the series examine heritage and tourism, and their relationships to local community, economic development, regional ecology, heritage conservation and preservation, and related indigenous, regional, and national political and cultural issues.

Titles in series:

Speaking for the Enslaved
Heritage Interpretation at Antebellum Plantation Sites
Antoinette T. Jackson

Faith in Heritage
Displacement, Development, and Religious Tourism in Contemporary China
Robert J. Shepherd

Haunted Heritage
The Cultural Politics of Ghost Tourism, Populism, and the Past
Michele Hanks

The Political Museum
Power, Conflict, and Identity in Cyprus
Theopisti Stylianou-Lambert and Alexandra Bounia

Culture, Celebrity, and the Cemetery
Hollywood Forever
Linda Levitt

Series page: https://www.routledge.com/Heritage-Tourism-and-Community/book-series/HTAC

Culture, Celebrity, and the Cemetery

Hollywood Forever

Linda Levitt

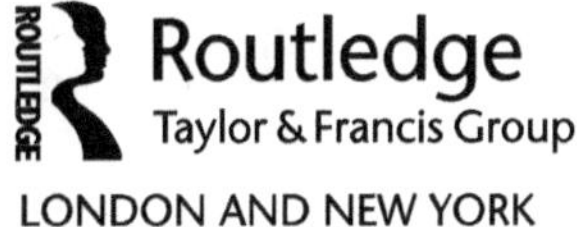

LONDON AND NEW YORK

First published 2018 by Routledge

2 Park Square, Milton Park, Abingdon, Oxon OX14 4RN
605 Third Avenue, New York, NY 10017

Routledge is an imprint of the Taylor & Francis Group, an informa business

First issued in paperback 2021

Publisher's Note

The publisher has gone to great lengths to ensure the quality of this reprint but points out that some imperfections in the original copies may be apparent.

Library of Congress Cataloging-in-Publication Data
A catalog record for this book has been requested

ISBN: 978-1-138-60978-5 (hbk)
ISBN: 978-0-367-52121-9 (pbk)

Typeset in Times New Roman
by Apex CoVantage, LLC

Contents

Preface

Hollywood is one of the most famous places in America. Its hillside sign is iconic. *La La Land* almost won the Academy Award for Best Picture in 2017. One of the most hilarious sequences of episodes in the beloved *I Love Lucy* comedy series takes place in Hollywood with an array of stars. But where did all those celebrities go? In other words, what happened on the other side of fame?

In this tremendously original monograph Linda Levitt presents Hollywood's cemetery of the stars—the Hollywood Forever Cemetery—as a place of popular culture and cultural memory, as well as a variant of America's cemetery landscapes. It is predictably a place of commemoration and last respects (and the only cemetery actually in Hollywood), but unlike other cemeteries the vast majority of visitors to this cemetery are typically unrelated to the members of the mortuary community interred there. Rather, they are fan tourists and, remarkably, they are devoted to people long dead, such a Rudolph Valentino who died in 1926.

Integrating close reading of theoretical literature on memorials, place making, construction of identity, tourism, and dark tourism, Dr. Levitt argues for the generation of a sense of personal closeness to the celebrities, an engagement and experience that enriches the tourist's knowledge and understanding of the world of cinema and of the past as an eternal present thanks to technology.

From a cemetery that was in such utter disrepair and bankrupt in the 1970s, 1980s, and 1990s that it was on the verge of being condemned, Hollywood Forever was purchased by new owners in 1998 and has been reborn under that management. It is now a brilliant success with tours, an outdoor film series, concerts, comedy performances, and commemorative events. It has rapidly evolved to reflect and utilize the technology of these times. Not only can one visit the cemetery's tangible space, but Hollywood Forever has also created a strong cyber presence with "Life Stories" that honor more than one hundred celebrities. Combined with TCM/Turner Classic Movies, new publics are being formed to learn about and remember the Hollywood of old in the social and political context of American society in each decade of the twentieth century.

Beyond being a description and critical analysis of this fascinating cemetery as a landscape of famous death, Dr. Levitt coherently weaves the theme of cultural memory and meaning making throughout each chapter. She highlights creative new strategies of commemoration that are ensuring the viability and relevance of Hollywood Forever Cemetery in today's times. Unmoored from staid traditions, the celebration of life overtakes mourning at Hollywood Forever Cemetery as the cemetery successfully presents itself as an exciting attraction for multiple new communities and a venue for new performances while safeguarding and promoting this famous aspect of American cultural heritage.

Helaine Silverman
Series Editor

1 Introduction

Locating Cultural Memory

Monuments and memorials to the dead and past events are scattered across the built landscape of America. They are especially important today, an era in which many are driven to record, commemorate, and archive the events of their lives, both personal and cultural (Doss, 2010; Zerubavel, 2003). The digital revolution has created easy documentation opportunities and expansive storage, enabling one to create a personal archive of one's life, including both personal experiences and cultural artifacts that have meanings attached to them. Such archives range from personal photographs and video to recorded film, television, and music. Thus, the past is especially personal and accessible, and as such it changes relationships with memory and history. As individuals engage in these archival activities, they mark new territories in the relationship between personal memory and cultural memory.

In their research, historians Roy Rozenweig and David Thelen (1998) discovered that history matters, significantly, to people in the United States. Yet history matters in ways that are personal rather than necessarily being patriotically attached to the nation-state. Seeking out historical knowledge is about finding ways to situate oneself in the world. What is my relationship to my community? How do I belong? Visitors can form a temporary bond with strangers when they stand together at the Vietnam Veterans Memorial or at the Strawberry Fields[1] memorial in Central Park, as well as spontaneous memorials that take form in the aftermath of tragic events. Bearing witness may be significant because it allows one to join together with others in a shared experience. Feeling oneself as part of the history of a community to which you belong—local, national, cultural, or otherwise—is a fundamental reason to engage with history and cultural memory.

In her work on public memory and commemoration, Erika Doss (2010) proposes the idea that the United States is engaged in a practice of "memorial mania" marked by a driven and determined need to commemorate. Doss argues that the "excessive, frenzied, and extreme" proliferation of memorials is drawn from a pressing need to create material "repositories of feelings and emotions" (p. 13). Doss's argument for a need to physically manifest our cultural traumas and triumphs is accompanied by an ephemeral sense of reality. A culture that contends with an overabundance of news and information is also subject to the feeling of one crisis rushing up on the heels of another, making it difficult to mark any particular moments as relatively more significant than the last. Those who have a personal connection to or investment in an event will store the relevant digital artifacts on a private hard drive or cloud memory, an act of preservation that is also one of isolation. The tendency to hoard digital photos, video, and articles that tie the individual to the event is a private endeavor, and because digital storage can be rendered invisible (in contrast with magazines, newspaper clippings, and printed photographs), they are easily forgotten. French historian Pierre Nora (1999) puts this dilemma in the contrast between memory and history. He notes that the "fear that everything is on the verge of disappearing, coupled with the anxiety about the precise significance of the present and uncertainty about the future, invests even the humblest testimony, the most modest vestige, with the dignity of being potentially memorable" (pp. 296–298). Unable to determine what should be saved, the default response is to save everything in the hope that something will eventually be valuable. Part of the impulse to create memorials is to insure that important public events are not forgotten. The built memorial also functions importantly on one hand to create a means for individuals to tie themselves to events, and on the other hand to create a physical place that represents people or events, enabling and promoting shared commemoration.

The touristic visit or pilgrimage to the cemetery can be, like the visit to a sanctioned memorial, a means of stitching oneself into the cultural past. This book considers the articulation and performance of commemoration in contemporary culture, specifically situated at Hollywood Forever. Because of the public figures who are interred there, Hollywood Forever functions as a site of pilgrimage for fans and as a tourist attraction for those with an interest in the various histories that are represented at the cemetery. Each chapter examines how the cemetery leverages its rich resources from the past to generate new collective experiences and attitudes in the present.

Through the outdoor film series Cinespia, a community-wide Día de los Muertos celebration, and annual memorial services and commemorative events, Hollywood Forever invites visitors to use the cemetery as social space. In examining the rituals and performances surrounding celebrity fan culture, this book looks as how fandom creates a sense of community that is deeply connected to the physical space of Hollywood Forever. Using the space of the cemetery for entertainment and leisure has the potential to change perceptions of the cemetery as uneasiness with the setting fades and visitors become comfortable and enjoy their experience. As Hollywood Forever functions as a space that can provide both solitude and community, perceptions of the cemetery change in the process.

Cultural Memory

As sociologist Eviatar Zerubavel (2003) points out, cultural memory is "more than just an aggregate of individuals' personal memories" but rather comprises what a group, culture, or nation "*collectively* considers historically eventful" (p. 28, emphasis original). Where some instances of personal memory are performative, individuals who participate in acts of memory collectively are marking an event as significant. Commemoration becomes an event in itself. The nascent field of memory studies shows that people want to participate in making history. In an era of media convergence and access to extensive archival and contemporary media, people do this by creating documents, websites, and YouTube videos. They post Tweets, write blogs, and update their status messages, all means of one-to-many communication that becomes a part of public discourse, no matter how insignificant individual voices may be. Individuals participating in social media want to be stitched in—they want theirs to be one of the voices that is heard and represented on the landscape of cultural memory.

A similar perspective from Svetlana Boym (2001) places memory first in the quotidian. She writes of her own work in studying the former Soviet Union that "collective memory will be understood here as the common landmarks of everyday life. They constitute shared social frameworks of individual recollections" (p. 53). While on the one hand there is a desire to capture the present and sanctify it by transforming into a medium like a photograph, a status message, or a file that can be stored and saved, there is on the other hand the everyday movement through the world that is at the heart of what constitutes cultural memory. What is recalled and brought back through nostalgia and retro movements are not only groundbreaking and catastrophic events, but also the coffee mugs, the fashions, and certainly the films that were commonplace and taken for granted in their time.

Cultural memory is not merely a matter of looking back to the past, but rather looking back with a purpose—to reify, to restore, to transform, or to otherwise use the past to serve purposes for the present. Cultural memory is comprised of stories and images that communities and individuals hold up to remind themselves of who they are. By sifting through both personal and cultural memories, individuals work to create a narrative of a world they wish to belong to while also remaking, or choosing to ignore, the stories and images that conflict with a desired worldview.

Public monuments, memorials, and cemeteries are material articulations of that narrative in the realm of cultural memory. Communication scholar Barbie Zelizer (1995) asserts that cultural memory is concerned with "the establishment of social identity, authority, solidarity, and political affiliation" rather than with historical accuracy (p. 217). Visiting sites of cultural memory is a way to set into motion the relationship between the present and the past. Activating the past by remembering people, events, disasters, and celebrations works to establish group and community formation. Memorials often serve to form communities of like-minded individuals who remember together, building cultural significance through the value of collective memory. Such acts of forming community can also be a means of exclusion, as is often seen in acts of commemoration where some individuals feel the performance of memory does not represent their position. The addition of statuary at the Vietnam Veterans Memorial and the bitter infighting among family members, first responders, and other stakeholders at the September 11 Memorial & Museum are recent examples.

Many contemporary cemeteries eschew monuments, preferring the serene visage of a lawn park, intended to soothe grieving visitors. The even, undisturbed grassy field of the lawn park does not allow for creative memorials, yet the historical cemeteries that draw tourists typically include a variety of evocative gravesites.

Cemeteries

As cities and towns reinvent themselves as tourist attractions, cemeteries, with their inherent historical value, are an obvious draw for heritage tourism sites. Yet the cultural role of the cemetery is complex and varied. While it can be a place of daytime serenity and reflection for some visitors, the cemetery at night has long been characterized culturally as a site of fear and gloom. Whether one visits the cemetery on a ghost tour or with a small group of friends, there is some pleasure to be gained from the daring adventure of being in a foreboding, or perhaps forbidden, place at night. Popular culture has leveraged this fear through frightening stories set in the cemeteries of folklore, fiction, and film. For many, the proximity to the dead is enough of a discomfort to make the cemetery an unpleasant place. Some are uncomfortable with the idea of being surrounded by corpses, while others avoid the cemetery to avoid confronting the inevitability of their own death.

Cultural perspectives on the cemetery are as diverse as culture itself, and the relationships individuals have with cemeteries are influenced by an array of factors such as religious beliefs and upbringing, attitudes toward death, and personal experience. Children who grow up having family photographs made on Daffodil Sunday at Cleveland's Lake View cemetery, for example, will have their attitude shaped by participating in an enjoyable outdoor celebration at the cemetery. Many others only pass through the cemetery gates in a state of grief, attending the funeral of a loved one and hesitating to visit the gravesite on subsequent occasions because the memory associated with that place seems irreconcilably sad.

While discomfort with the cemetery is more common than not, this was not always the case. Two acts of separation mark the changing cultural outlook toward the cemetery: the removal of the dying and the dead from the home and the relocation of the dead to the outskirts of the city. In his work on heterotopias, Michel Foucault (1986) marks the shift in attitude toward the cemetery as one that accompanies a geographical shift: the relocation of cemeteries outside of the city, which became common practice at the beginning of the nineteenth century, separated the living from the dead. Foucault describes the cemetery as a paradoxical "other space." Deeply connected to familial and cultural life "since each individual, each family has relatives in the cemetery," it is also detached from the processes of everyday life and physically removed on the landscape (p. 25). Establishing new cemeteries on the outskirts of the city was part of urban growth in the United States in the 1820s and 1830s and marked a significant shift in burial practices. In her extensive study of cemetery history, *Silent City on a Hill: Landscapes of Memory and Boston's Mount Auburn Cemetery*, Blanche Linden-Ward (1989) describes burial reform at that time as "only one of many ways in which urbanites attempted to improve their surroundings" (p. 149); enhancing the conditions of graveyards was part of the overall growth and transformation of urban life. The overcrowded graveyard as the source of a pungent stench stemming from the decay of corpses buried there certainly contributed to the sense of the cemetery as a fearful place, even after more sanitary and pleasant facilities were built. Rather than being a place to mourn, the graveyard was a place to avoid.

Mount Auburn Cemetery was established in 1831 to stem controversy over burial practices in Boston. It was the first of the so-called "rural cemeteries," and it marks a shift in the lexicon from "graveyard" to "cemetery," denoting "the Greek word for 'sleeping chamber' because they were considered temporary resting places during the wait for Judgment Day." Located in neighboring Cambridge, the cemetery was well removed from the urban center of Boston at the time of its founding. Mount Auburn served as the model for many other new cemeteries throughout the country. The rural cemetery is designed to combine the aesthetics of the natural environment with neatly-planned and organized plots, resulting in a garden-like setting. As such, the cemetery began to take on new purposes. Stanley French (1974) explains that in the rural cemetery "the plenitude and beauties of nature combined with art would convert the graveyard from a shunned place of horror into an enchanting place of succor and instruction" (pp. 46–47). As an "enchanting place," the rural cemetery also became leisure space, a location for strolling along shaded paths and picnicking, before the development of city parks allowed citizens to escape the noise and chaos of city life. Cemeteries provided the primary space available for enjoying the outdoors in an urban context. Similarly, the monuments and artworks located in rural cemeteries offered the public access to art before museums were established. Nonetheless, those who saw the cemetery as a sacred place were irritated by visitors who came only to enjoy it for strolling and relaxation. These conflicts have been revived as Hollywood Forever and other cemeteries host cultural events.

The rural cemetery design led to a new kind of overcrowding—the overwhelming number of trees, shrubs, and monuments created visual clutter as well as high maintenance costs for mowing and upkeep. The cemeteries also faced overcrowding from visitors. Historian David Sloane notes that the rural cemeteries were early tourist attractions for casual visitors and guided tours, creating noise and obstruction for mourners. Philadelphia's Laurel Hill Cemetery, the second such cemetery to be developed, saw as many as 140,000 visitors in 1860. In response to the concern about congestion, landscape architect Adolphe Strauch created the first lawn park cemetery in 1855 at Spring Grove in Cincinnati, minimizing the landscape elements and prohibiting fencing of individual gravesites. The result is a more placid environment, focused on uniformity and cleanliness rather than a lush natural setting. Hollywood Forever's official directory (2006) describes the cemetery as a lawn park: "spacious, simple, pastoral landscapes would be complemented by elegant monuments and markers, combining art and nature in a beautiful park-like setting" (p. 2). Where public parks began to take over some of the greenspace functions of cemeteries at the turn of the last century, now Hollywood Forever is drawing people to the paths and gardens on the grounds. Visitors stroll through the cemetery and are welcome to do so.

The cemetery is a temporal refuge as well. Entering this isolated space can function as an escape from the crisis time of the present into a variety of pasts that can be rendered as more romantic, more idealized, or simpler than life is now. This kind of nostalgia is, as geographer Karen Till (2005) posits, "often motivated by a desire to replace apprehension about change in the present and future through the pleasures of remembering a known place in the past" (p. 57). Cemeteries are locations outside of place and time, and frequent visitors develop a strong sense of place that creates feelings of familiarity and comfort. It may seem paradoxical that a place where one goes to grieve, or may choose to avoid because of the grief associated with it, can be a place of comfort. Spending time tending to the grave of a loved one is a way of spending time with memories of that person, opening oneself to the pleasure of remembering that may be mingled with a profound sense of loss. Through that commingling, however, healing and a sense of acceptance about the inevitability of loss and death are possible.

Cemeteries and Commemoration

History finds a home in cemeteries that are visited as sites of commemoration. Arlington National Cemetery, for example, claims four million visitors a year, as individuals and families travel to Washington to perform acts of personal and cultural memory. Whether to watch the ritual changing of the guard at the Tomb of the Unknowns, to pay respect at the gravesite of John F. Kennedy, marked by an eternal flame, or to honor a family member or loved one interred at Arlington, the gravesite pilgrimage is not an uncommon cultural event. Yet these pilgrimages do not always involve national pride—as the visits to Marilyn Monroe's grave in Los Angeles or to Elvis Presley's burial site at Graceland indicate, fandom is also a common drive to commemoration. As the final resting place of celebrities and notable public figures such as silent film star Rudolph Valentino, actor Mel Blanc, best known for voicing Bugs Bunny, and Estelle Getty of *Golden Girls* fame, Hollywood Forever Cemetery has long served as a tourist attraction and a site of public memory. Valentino's gravesite in the Cathedral Mausoleum exemplifies both the ritual and performative nature of commemoration. Since his untimely death in 1926, fans, film stars, and friends have made an annual pilgrimage for Valentino's memorial service at Hollywood Forever. This tradition continued even when the cemetery suffered from neglect in the aftermath of the 1994 Northridge earthquake,[2] when broken tombstones, shattered stained glass windows, and lack of upkeep drew the cemetery closer to its eventual bankruptcy. In that bleak setting, mourning was perhaps a more prominent feeling than celebration for Valentino's life and career. Yet such mourning would be tinged with nostalgia not only for the actor, but also for the long history of memorial services in his honor and the touch of glamour that once accompanied them. Going to the cemetery to remember Valentino, and to remember the glamour of the silent film era, enables visitors to participate in an act of cultural memory defined by coming together to commemorate the past. Individuals who participate in acts of memory collectively are marking an event as significant. Commemoration becomes an event in itself.

No monument or memorial can represent the individual memory of everyone who feels connected to it. Visiting a site like a cemetery welcomes a polysemic experience—along with spaces of mourning are spaces of leisure and reflection. The variety of memorial markers at Hollywood Forever includes aesthetically appealing memorials, some of which are solemn and monumental while others are lighthearted, reflecting ways in which both the dead and their loved ones want them to be remembered. Notions of solemnity that one might carry to a cemetery are undone at Hollywood Forever. The cemetery is unusual with regard to its long history of allowing unique memorials rather than the flush-to-the-ground, standardized grave markers common in most lawn parks. These memorial markers can provide an emotional structure for public memory, by both literally and metaphorically containing such memories.

Visiting the Dead

Erika Doss (2010) argues that memorials play a central cultural role by drawing visitors into relationship with the national consciousness: "For Americans, the touristic experience of visiting them, whether as an obligatory civic exercise in middle school or while on family vacation, is a primary means of learning about and becoming an emotionally engaged member of the nation" (p. 56). That a visit to a memorial invites emotional engagement shows the ideological, as well as personal, significance of such sites. The tension between history and memory demands that personal memory be carefully tended, and that individuals and groups continue to work to imbue places with meaning that can open the dialogue between the past and the present. Living in a culture where the idea of history erodes memory through the act of creating official, sanctioned versions of the collective past renders individuals less capable of finding the past to be of personal value. History becomes someone else's story. Doss sees the difference as a shift from passive knowledge to experiential knowledge and notes that experience is facilitated by artists and architects who create memorial sites that welcome it. She refers to Maya Lin, best known for designing the Vietnam Veterans Memorial, who said "I don't make objects; I make places. I think that is very important—the places set the stage for experience and for understanding experience" (Doss, 2010, p. 51).

Maya Lin's choice of black granite for the Vietnam Veterans Memorial was widely misunderstood by those who called the design for the memorial "a black gash of shame." She did not see black as a color, but as a reflective surface. "Reflective" here has manifold meaning—Lin knew that visitors looking at the memorial would not only see rows upon rows of names, they would also see their own image reflected back to them. The confluence of the self and the memorial can lead the visitor to reflect on his relationship to death, to war, to the names of the dead. The reflection is also hopeful—beyond the image of one's own face are the open sky, perhaps a banner of clouds running through it, and people standing and walking along the memorial's walls, reinscribing the connection between self and other.

Sanctioned memorials mark and redefine public space for commemorative practices. In some instances, memorials are located at the site of a disaster, such as the Oklahoma City National Memorial and the National September 11 Memorial & Museum at the site of the former World Trade Center. Others memorials are strategically placed in public spaces established for commemoration, like the National Mall in Washington, DC. Yet some places, like the *Flamme de Liberté* monument near the Alma Tunnel where Lady Diana Spencer died, become significant sites of memory without being sanctioned memorials. The Lorraine Motel in Memphis, where Martin Luther King, Jr. was killed on the balcony in 1968, was not marked as an officially sanctioned site until twenty-three years later, when the motel became home to the National Civil Rights Museum.[3] Other sites serve as the destination for pilgrimages on the anniversaries of celebrity deaths; examples include Jim Morrison's grave in Père Lachaise cemetery in Paris as well as Dealey Plaza, the site of John F. Kennedy's assassination. These gatherings are not official, organized, or scripted events but rather mark the gesture of publicly acknowledging a cultural loss by situating oneself at a site of tragedy.

Cemeteries are more significantly sites of personal or individual memory than cultural memory, yet at Hollywood Forever, visitors feel connected to celebrities through their stardom. Like a site of tragedy, the celebrity cemetery enables a sense of who is buried there and becomes a site of cultural memory as well. Unlike most cemeteries, but similar to many sanctioned memorials, Hollywood Forever is a tourist attraction. As the final resting place of many celebrities, visitors are drawn to the cemetery to remember people they did not know but feel they can get closer to the famous person, if only by virtue of his or her material remains.

Hollywood Tourism

Tourism is not a passive activity. Daniel Boorstin (1962) wrote in his historical comparison between the traveler and the tourist that tourists observed foreign places from a safe distance—on a bus, in a group, with a tour guide to interpret their experience, and with the camera lens creating a filter between the tourist and his or her surrounding reality. Tourism today has a radically different map, aligned with shifts in perceptions of history. Visitors want engagement and experience, a desire produced largely by the multi-billion dollar tourism industry that promises transformative events for visitors. As the largest global industry, travel and tourism accounts for 9.4 percent of world's gross domestic product, the equivalent of US$7.2 trillion. One of out of every eleven jobs worldwide is associated with the travel and tourism industry. These numbers reveal as much about cultures and they do about the economy. There is a deep engagement with knowing, understanding, and experiencing the world, both local and at a distance.

Sociologist John Urry coined the term "the tourist gaze" to describe the kinds of looking that visitors do in unfamiliar places that are othered and visually objectified. Yet even the familiar can be made strange, as Urry and his collaborators note that tourism "incorporates mindsets and performances that transform places of the humdrum and ordinary into the apparently spectacular and exotic" (Baerenholdt, Haldrup, and Urry, 2004, p. 2). The images that fall under the tourist gaze are reified and repeated—in postcards, films, and elsewhere—and become the sought-after sites that confirm a tourist's encounter with place. Of note is that the tourist gaze is no more complex than a particular way of seeing that can be called upon in any instance; it is a learned practice. For local residents to frequently visit the same memorial or memory site may mean that it is a taken for granted part of the landscape or that it becomes connected to an individual's sense of self. Los Angeles offers iconic buildings like the Capitol Records building or the Chinese Theatre as examples of places that might readily draw the tourist gaze, even when the locale is part of everyday experience. Yet how tourist locations take on meaning is idiosyncratic, as the experience of the tourist is always contingent upon on the individual and her life experiences. If, for example, a fan of the *Harry Potter* films were to visit the Chinese Theatre forecourt and locate the handprints and footprints of the films' lead actors, the visit to Hollywood Boulevard would resonate more significantly than it would for a tourist who finds no personal connection.

The circulation of histories from various perspectives makes clear that the interaction of personal memory and cultural memory is ongoing. This is especially poignant in a place like Los Angeles, where Hollywood's history is tightly bound to the personal memories of individual audience members and fans. Hollywood is the focal point for cinema's cultural history. A particular history of cinema is told through iconic photographs and video footage of celebrities living their glamorous lives in the palatial mansions of Beverly Hills, the clubs and restaurants of the city, and the celebrations of red carpet stardom at destinations like the Chinese Theatre. Hollywood's history, and its reality, are both far more nuanced, yet its tourism is steeped in nostalgia for an enchanting and celebrated past when both movies and the stars who appeared in them seemed magical. The public's relationship to both celebrities and film changed with the focus on "behind the scenes" content. Where journalists were once often complicit in protecting the potentially scandalous behavior of stars, from Rock Hudson's homosexuality to Judy Garland's alcoholism, the era of the exposé that began with *Lifestyles of the Rich and Famous* and *People* magazine rendered the idealization of the celebrity difficult to maintain. Furthermore, production footage released ahead of a film's completion, along with on-the-set reporting and the subsequent DVD extras, disclose the techniques of filmmaking that once made movies seem extraordinary.

Tourists who bring an interest in the entertainment industry to their time in Los Angeles seek an experience of celebrity culture. Studio tours offer a behind-the-scenes pleasure of authenticity for film and television fans, along with the potential for spotting a celebrity on the grounds. Thousands of tourists each year choose to include a tour of movie stars' homes as part of their Hollywood vacation. The iconic tour provider, Starline Tours, has its main terminal at the Chinese Theatre, itself central to a visit to Hollywood Boulevard. Tourists enjoy the opportunity to get as close as possible to the physical presence of the famous by literally standing in their footsteps. The aura of celebrity is vibrant in the forecourt, as film fans can easily recall the opening night premieres at the Chinese Theatre over decades past.

The theater officially opened on May 18, 1927, a few weeks after the first footprint ceremony, honoring Mary Pickford and Douglas Fairbanks, Sr. Pickford and Fairbanks were partners in the theater, along with Sid Grauman and Howard Schenck. When Ted Mann purchased the theater in 1973, the name was changed to Mann's Chinese Theatre until 2001, when the original name was restored. In 2013, Chinese television manufacturer TCL purchased naming rights for the theater, adding yet another new designation to the culturally significant space. Despite these changes, the theater, rich in movie history, is still sought after by studios for Hollywood premieres. Adjacent to the Chinese Theatre are the first stars dedicated on the Hollywood Walk of Fame, which claims to attract more than nine million tourists a year. But it was not always this way.

Hollywood's deep ties to cinema persisted even as the movie capital fell into decline. As audiences turned from film to television in the 1950s, their attention also turned away from Hollywood as a tourist destination. Television studios moved from Hollywood to Burbank in the 1960s, and a downward spiral began as the elite left Hollywood. Restaurants, bars, and retailers struggled to stay afloat. The 1994 Northridge earthquake and the damage left in its wake might have been the end of Hollywood had ambitious developers, along with those who maintained an idealized view of Hollywood's sense of place, not been willing to invest in redefining Hollywood Boulevard and the surrounding area in the public imagination. In 1998, as construction was beginning on the Hollywood & Highland Center, *Newsweek* reported:

> Seven million tourists a year flock to Hollywood Boulevard hoping for a whiff of the film capital's glamorous past. They check out the stars' footprints at Mann's Chinese Theater, stroll the Walk of Fame—and

> leave. For decades, the area has been home to tattoo parlors and T-shirt shops; hookers compete for corners with crack addicts. A recent study revealed that the average tourist retreats to his air-conditioned bus in a mere 20 minutes.
>
> (p. 90)

The 1999 edition of the *Time Out Los Angeles* guide concurred with *Newsweek*, warning tourists away from Hollywood with some of the same colorful descriptions: "You can see glimpses of what Hollywood Boulevard used to be in the wonderfully opulent facades of Mann's Chinese Theater and El Capitan Theater, but these days the famous street is just a dirty and depressing stretch of boarded-up storefronts, tacky souvenir shops and teenage runaways with Mohican haircuts" (p. 61). These negative critiques of Hollywood coincided with the beginning of the area's resurrection, led by the Disney Corporation's renovation and reopening of El Capitan Theatre in 1991. The nearby Egyptian Theatre, across Hollywood Boulevard from the Chinese Theatre, was a Hollywood mainstay from its opening in 1922 until it was finally closed in 1992. The nonprofit organization American Cinematheque purchased the building from the city for $1, then invested $15 million to renovate and restore the theatre. Development of the W Hollywood Hotel at Hollywood and Vine as well as construction of the upscale Hollywood & Highland Center and its Kodak Theater, which now hosts the Academy Awards, secured a turning point for Hollywood as a safer, family-oriented destination. That Disney's restoration of El Capitan was one of the early revitalization projects leads easily to discussion of the Disneyfication of Hollywood. The transformation of Times Square offers a quick corollary for how removing urban blight can also strip a commercial area of its character. Scott Michaels (personal communication, August 26, 2006), founder of Dearly Departed Tours,[4] offers one such critique:

> The Chinese Theatre is such a magical place. What I like doing is I go out, and when I'm coming home I pass the Chinese Theatre at like one or two in the morning and I can go all by myself in the forecourt. It's my favorite place in the world. I love the Chinese Theatre. Again, I feel possessive of it. Because those of us who never left it, now feel like we're not welcome. Because it's become trendy, and the trendy crowd has sort of embraced it, you know?

At the same time, whitewashing the historical district creates a clean slate for tourists to engage a limitless number of pasts for Hollywood. When audiences look back on the past, they see pieces of themselves. Memory is a performative endeavor, and through remembering, visitors build a sense of identity based on the elements of the cultural past that they select to carry away and carry forward with them. These elements are referenced repeatedly through choices made in selecting souvenirs, displaying artifacts of one's travels, and posting photographs, images, or messages on social media sites. In these ways, tourism acts as a powerful site of identity creation.

Cultural memory also figures significantly in identity creation, as an individual's response to a cultural event—tragedy, celebration, and everyday occurrences—shapes attitudes about self and other. Cultural memory is in part constituted through media, and for celebrity culture that includes film, television, print, and digital media. Celebrity is also a site of identification and meaning-making, and the public spaces of Hollywood manifest those meanings. What is remembered is not necessarily one's own individual past, but a cultural past that enables identity formation, optimism, and longing. Nora (1989) argues that history is "the reconstruction, always problematic and incomplete, of what is no longer. Memory is always a phenomenon of the present, a bond tying us to the eternal present; history is a representation of the past" (p. 9). From Nora's perspective, memorials are unnecessary as sites of commemoration when we instead immortalize the everyday by investing it with meaning because of its associations. Landmarks that are still used, lived-in spaces are imbued with meaning because the city is a palimpsest. Historical tours and informed tourists are aware of the history of a particular street corner or hotel lobby, and standing in that space can give the visitor a connection between past and present. These ideas are fundamental to tourism and to the thinking that helped drive the renovation and restoration of Hollywood landmarks.

To think of cultural memory as textual, architectural, discursive, and fluid enables Hollywood to provide a backdrop for much of celebrity culture and how it is remembered. Through tourism and film as nostalgic practices, culture holds on to Hollywood. The city is a center of nostalgia, not only for aging cinephiles, but also for young audience members caught up in a passion for the more recent films they have enjoyed, whether on home video or at the IMAX or multiplex.

At the Heart of Hollywood: Hollywood Forever

As a site of public memory, Hollywood Forever lends itself readily to acts of commemoration, whether organized or spontaneous. Many organized events at Hollywood Forever are the result of the cemetery's efforts to regain both its business and its cultural capital. There is something seemingly paradoxical about the rebirth of a cemetery, yet the story of Hollywood Forever is one of resurrection. Purchased out of bankruptcy by Forever Enterprises in 1998, the cemetery had lost its glamorous image as the final resting place of Hollywood legends from cinema's early years. Due to embezzlement and neglect by its former manager, the cemetery required an estimated $7 million investment to repair damages and refurbish the buildings and grounds. Cemeterian Tyler Cassity wanted not only to restore the cemetery, but also to transform the death care industry. Cassity espouses the idea of celebrating life rather than mourning death and encourages this shift in cultural perspectives by inviting the use of the cemetery as leisure space. Hollywood Forever leverages its rich resources from the past to generate new collective experiences and attitudes in the present. While events like Cinespia and the Dia de los Muertos celebration get penciled in on Angelinos' annual calendars, the cemetery also hosts yoga classes, performances of Shakespeare plays, poetry readings, and comedy. These events turn the cemetery into a welcoming social space.

The focus on lives lived is also reinforced by LifeStories, the digital memorials produced by Forever Enterprises. Beyond their primary use as tributes shown as part of a funeral service, LifeStories are available for viewing online in the Library of Lives. Photographs, video, music, and personal recollections are combined into a video tribute for the funeral and beyond. In a 2000 episode from National Public Radio's "This American Life," host Ira Glass gently pokes fun at his own cultural traditions to show how LifeStories can have a transformative effect on grieving:

> On screen are pictures of the deceased—black and white on the beach as a young man, a wedding shot with his wife, the obligatory goofy shot of him in a dress with his buddies. The photos were selected by the family and set to a musical soundtrack, which was also selected by the family. These being Jews, my people, as you might guess, there is only one choice about the music. Really, no choice at all. Barbra. Auntie Viv audibly exclaims, "Oy vey!" Grandma Goldie responds, "Oy Viv." But here's the thing, people are crying. They're crying more than they did during the eulogies. Later, after the burial, back at the house everyone watches the video over and over. They laugh, they cry, they rewind, they replay. Barbra hasn't had a hit like this since *Yentl.*

Glass shows how funeral practices can be transformed when mourners are given the opportunity to reminisce about the life experiences of the deceased, celebrating the milestones as well as the everyday.

More than 4,000 Lifestories are included in the Library of Lives. Some pay tribute to the dead while others are works in progress, put together by individuals who have purchased pre-need burial sites at Hollywood Forever. As the shift in cultural attitudes toward death in the United States sees individuals often taking a more proactive role in making their own funeral arrangements, LifeStories enables people to tell their own stories of how they want to be remembered. Hollywood Forever also created a series of LifeStories to honor more than 100 well-known public figures interred at the cemetery. These videos not only serve as aspirational models for new LifeStories, but also build the cultural capital of Hollywood Forever's celebrity status.

The inclusion of celebrity LifeStories on the cemetery's website is one means of extending tourists' interests in visiting Hollywood Forever to pay tribute firsthand. As the premier cemetery in Hollywood during the 1920s, Hollywood Forever counts among its interments celebrities who are considered notorious because of their involvement in scandals of murder, sex, and drugs that made headlines in Hollywood's Golden Age. Virginia Rappe, the subject of one of the most lurid sex scandals of the era, is buried in the Garden of Legends. Rappe died following a party hosted by Roscoe "Fatty" Arbuckle, one of the highest paid and most popular actors of his time. He was tried and acquitted for her rape and murder and was never able to recover from the damage done to his reputation. This story is often circulated among visitors to Hollywood Forever, whether on an official tour of the grounds, a haunted history tour, or among those with an interest in the celebrity cemetery. Activated by the material evidence of history, Rappe's story exemplifies cultural memory as dialogic. While the physical presence of the memorial site does work to sustain a sense of the past, understandings of and relationship to the past change over time. Engagement with places of memory can lead to a shift in the meaning of past events and individuals—spending time at the cemetery, talking with others about the people buried there, and participating in commemorative events—enable the past to be reconsidered and reconstituted in the present. In seeing sites of memory as dialogic, communication scholar Bradford Vivian (2004) argues that "an official site of public memory—a monument, an archive, or sacred ground—represents not the static container of such memory, but the dynamic reference point for the diverse memory work that sustains it, the commemorative nexus formed at the intersection of a public's many mnemonic practices" (p. 203). The sheer number of individuals who visit cemeteries, whether to engage in personal or cultural memory, indicates that conversations with the past are ongoing. The cemetery is a space in which, inspired by the surroundings, conversation about the past can occur. For a visitor interested in history, the cemetery can be a place to continue a conversation with the past already underway, enabling a material reference point for nostalgia, fandom, or history. Standing by the grave of actors from Hollywood's Golden Age, such as Tyrone Power or Marion Davies, is to situate oneself to tell, or to hear, a story that may not materialize in another way.

Places of memory can function to forestall forgetting and to prevent obsolescence. Cultural geographer J.B. Jackson (1980) points out that the "monument, in short, is a guide to the future: just as it confers a kind of immortality on the dead, it determines our actions for years to come" (p. 93). In order for a memorial to determine our actions, we must be able to respond to it, and the moment of reception must be taken seriously. Meanings are not universal, and neither is the response of the visitor. This is especially true of the cemetery in its roles as a site of both personal and cultural memory. At Hollywood Forever, even negative aspects of the past have been mobilized to reframe the cemetery's image. Hattie McDaniel, the actress who played Mammy in *Gone With the Wind*, was the first African-American to win an Academy Award. When McDaniel died in 1952, her wishes were to be buried at then-named Hollywood Memorial Park, in the company of other prominent Hollywood figures including Victor Fleming, who directed *Gone With the Wind*. Cemetery owner Jules Roth denied her request, as the cemetery had a "whites only" policy at the time. After purchasing the cemetery, Tyler Cassity offered a burial place for McDaniel, but her family chose not to have her disinterred and reburied, so a prominently situated cenotaph was dedicated in her honor instead. Paying tribute to Hattie McDaniel recalls not only *Gone With the Wind* and all that it invokes, but also recalls the cemetery's racism. In "righting that wrong," Cassity may intend to erase a racist past, but the gesture also creates a material reminder of it. Regardless of Cassity's intentions, how the memorial for McDaniel is understood rests with the visitor to the cemetery. If Hollywood Forever is working to change attitudes about death, the material artifacts of cultural memory—namely gravesites and memorial markers—are used in conjunction with organized events to create experiences that can evoke a desired perspective about our cultural past, transforming the cemetery from a place that is strictly solemn to one that can also invite celebration.

Hattie McDaniel is not the only celebrity honored but not buried at Hollywood Forever. After Jayne Mansfield's untimely death in 1967, a memorial service was held in Beverly Hills and her body was transported to Pennsylvania for interment. While Mansfield was known for her acting on stage and screen, she was also one of the early centerfold models for *Playboy*. Despite her intellect and skill, Mansfield was typecast, both in film and in her everyday reputation, as a "blonde bombshell," privileging her physical appearance over her other personal qualities. Despite her tragic death, and perhaps because of it, Jayne Mansfield has maintained an active community of fans. More than thirty years after her death, Mansfield's Los Angeles fan club dedicated a cenotaph for her at Hollywood Forever, giving them a place to gather and remember her. The cenotaph is engraved with the same language found on Mansfield's grave marker: "We live to love you more each day."

That Mansfield's fans felt compelled to create this site is testament to the power of place to situate and give voice to cultural memory.

Honorary cenotaphs for celebrities like McDaniel and Mansfield led fans of *The Wizard of Oz* to approach Hollywood Forever in 2011 with a request to create a memorial in honor of Toto, the beloved dog from the film. After her death, the Cairn terrier who played Toto was buried on her owner's ranch on land that was eventually paved over to become the Ventura Freeway. Hollywood Forever donated a premier plot of land at the corner of the Cathedral Mausoleum, just across from the cenotaph honoring Johnny Ramone. A bronze sculpture of Toto with an explanatory plaque is surrounded by flowers, honoring the memory of one of Hollywood's unique stars.

The desire to honor a celebrated figure by reburial or placement of a cenotaph within a cemetery has a long history. In *Digging Up the Dead*, Michael Kammen (2010) relates the campaign to disinter and move the remains of Edgar Allan Poe from an unmarked grave at Westminster Burial Ground to a more prominent, marked gravesite that attracts visitors to pay tribute to the writer. Kammen[5] argues that the "commercial desire to attract tourists and reasons rooted in local pride have also provided ongoing stimuli in the competition to possess or repossess the bodies of famous figures" (p. 23). The preceding examples demonstrate that the desire to commemorate a public figure, or to honor someone's last wishes, can also provide a passionate rationale for the desire to possess the bodies of famous figures. If Hollywood Forever is understood as a site that perpetuates cultural memory along with personal memory, it is worth noting that fan communities provided the impetus to honor both Jayne Mansfield and Toto. Further, to be in a space of memory invites commemoration. Hollywood Forever leverages its strong ties to celebrity to create activities that promote leisure and pleasure on the cemetery grounds. Through those activities, visitors develop a sense of connection with the cemetery and may imagine how they might incorporate their own acts of memory into its fabric. Several other events initiated by fans and friends of celebrities interred at Hollywood Forever perpetuate performances of cultural memory throughout the year.

Fans continue to commemorate Rudolph Valentino's death every August at Hollywood Forever, and for many years silent film fan Sparrow Morgan organized a birthday celebration for Douglas Fairbanks, Sr. that included a silent film screening at the cemetery. Each summer sees Linda Ramone host a tribute and cancer benefit in honor of her husband, the late Johnny Ramone. The benefit typically includes an array of celebrities from punk and rock music as well as actors like Nicholas Cage who were close friends of Ramone. These events give credence to the idea that history is constructed and that what aspects of the past are celebrated depend upon who has the resources to organize and promote such events. New burials, along with the ebb and flow of interest in entertainers and their productions, have resulted in changes to how the past is embraced at Hollywood Forever. By allowing visitors to wander the grounds, sharing anecdotes and making photographs, Hollywood Forever participates in the construction and reconstruction of cultural memory.

Preview

As a memory site, Hollywood Forever Cemetery in Los Angeles offers a place to consider memorialization and cultural memory while also looking closely at the articulation and performance of commemoration in contemporary culture. The remaining chapters of this book consider Hollywood Forever as a site of tourism and cultural memory from a variety of perspectives.

Chapter 2 situates Hollywood Forever in the context of the development of cemeteries in the United States. The chapter then addresses the ways that cemeteries generally and Hollywood Forever specifically serve as sites of cultural memory and are used as tourism destinations. A brief history of cemeteries in the United States and changing relationships with death over time provide insight into the unique qualities of Hollywood Forever.

Chapter 3 looks at the particular relationship between celebrity and cultural memory, considering the ways that tourists and fans are drawn to Hollywood Forever because of the celebrities who are interred at the cemetery. Through memorial celebrations and commemorative events for stars such as Rudolph Valentino and Johnny Ramone, Hollywood Forever becomes a site where fans gather, and return, taking photographs and leaving remembrances to demonstrate their ongoing involvement with the celebrities they admire. Due in part to the activities of tourists and fans, these stars remain in circulation in contemporary culture and are deployed as figures of cultural memory when meaning-making about the past is attached to their lives and creative work.

Cinespia, the outdoor film series at Hollywood Forever, is the focus of Chapter 4. Hollywood Forever has been the screening space for a popular outdoor movie series since 2002, when Cinespia began projecting films on the exterior wall of the Cathedral Mausoleum. Moviegoers at Cinespia create their own rituals as they gather with friends to establish their space on the Fairbanks Lawn with blankets, chairs, and elaborate picnic spreads. Being outdoors in open space eases some of the constraints of social decorum that dictates behavior in an indoor theater. This openness is enhanced by music and socializing before the screening, which evokes a more party-like atmosphere. By screening classic and contemporary cult films, Cinespia works to create new meaning for old films.

Chapter 5 analyzes the Día de los Muertos (Day of the Dead) celebration at the cemetery. Hollywood Forever Cemetery hosts one of the largest celebrations in the United States, and one of the few held at a U.S. cemetery. The event builds on the cemetery's own tradition of allowing creative methods of commemoration, such as evocative epitaphs and the inclusion of personal effects in memorial niches. The event also offers another means of engagement with celebrity culture, when altarists are remembering stars with whom they feel a deep sense of connection. The event is also used as a way to draw attention to forgotten actors interred at Hollywood Forever.

Finally, Chapter 6 looks broadly at the transformation of traditions at Hollywood Forever. From concerts on the Fairbanks Lawn to comedy performances at the historic Masonic Lodge on the cemetery grounds, Hollywood Forever continues to invite visitors for new experiences in a space often thought of as exclusive to mourners. Having always embraced a perspective that favors celebrating a life lived rather than mourning a loss, Hollywood Forever has played a role in recent transformations in death care, especially with regard to the good death movement. The cemetery's openness to fan communities has increased Hollywood Forever's significance as a tourist destination as well.

Notes

1 Yoko Ono, John Lennon's widow, has encouraged fans to gather in celebration of Lennon's birthday rather than on the anniversary of his death. The Strawberry Fields memorial in Central Park, which Ono helped design, was dedicated on what would have been Lennon's 45th birthday, October 9, 1985.

2 At a magnitude of 6.7, the January 17, 1994 earthquake resulted in 57 deaths and more than 9,000 injuries. Damages were estimated between $20 and $44 billion, the most costly earthquake in U.S. history.

3 For more on NCRM, see Bernard J. Armada's "Memory's Execution: (Dis)placing the Dissent Body" in *Places of Public Memory: The Rhetoric of Museums and Memorials* (2010), Dickinson, Blair, and Ott, Eds.

4 In addition to hosting tours that address the interests of dark tourism in Hollywood, in 2017 Michaels moved his operations to a location across from Hollywood Forever on Santa Monica Boulevard. The Dearly Departed Museum features memorabilia related to celebrity deaths. Its centerpiece is the crushed remains of the Buick Electra in which Jayne Mansfield died in a wreck in 1967. Tourists not familiar with Mansfield can connect to this dark history through Mansfield's daughter, actress Mariska Hargitay, who was also a passenger in the car. Hargitay and her brothers Miklos and Zoltan suffered only minor injuries.

5 Poe's grave is the site of a significant tradition, the appearance of the anonymous so-called "Poe Toaster" who would leave three roses and a partly-consumed bottle at Poe's grave on the anniversary of his death. This practice continued annually until 2010, when there was no visit. In a desire to sustain commemoration, the Maryland Historical Society chose a new, yet still anonymous Toaster to continue the tradition. Hollywood Forever has a similar history of the Lady in Black, who anonymously brought roses to the gravesite of Rudolph Valentino on the anniversary of his death. This tradition is discussed in greater detail in Chapter 3.

References

Baerenholdt, J. O., Haldrup, M. and Urry, J. (2004). *Performing tourist places*. London: Routledge.

Boym, S. (2001). *The future of nostalgia*. New York, NY: Basic Books.

Doss, E. (2010). *Memorial mania: Public feeling in America*. Chicago, IL: University of Chicago Press.

Foucault, M. (Spring 1986). *Of Other Spaces*. Trans. Jay Miskowiec. Diacritics 16.1, 22–27.

Jackson, J. B. (1980). *The necessity for ruins and other topics*. Amherst: University of Massachusetts Press.

Kammen, M. (2010). *Digging up the dead: A history of notable American reburials*. Chicago, IL: University of Chicago Press.

Linden-Ward, B. (1989). *Silent City on a Hill: Landscapes of Memory and Boston's Mount Auburn Cemetery*. Columbus: Ohio State University Press.

Mandala Research. (2013). *The cultural and heritage traveler: 2013 edition*. Alexandria, VA.

Nora, P. (1989). Between memory and history: Les lieux de memoire. *Representations*, 26, 7–24.

Nora, P. (1999). Memory is always suspect in the eyes of history. In Uwe Fleckner (Ed.), *The Treasure Chests of Mnemosyne: Selected Texts on Memory Theory from Plato to Derrida*. Newark, NJ: G&B International.

Rozenweig, R. and Thelen, D. (1998). *The presence of the past: Popular uses of history in American Life*. New York, NY: Columbia University Press.

Till, K. E. (2005). *The New Berlin: Memory, Politics, Space*. Minneapolis: University of Minnesota Press.

Time Out Los Angeles. (2nd ed.). (1999). Los Angeles, CA: Penguin.

Vivian, B. (2004). "A timeless now": Repetition and memory. In K. R. Phillps (Ed.), *Framing public memory* (pp. 187–211). Tuscaloosa, AL: University of Alabama Press.

Zelizer, B. (1995). Reading the past against the grain: The shape of memory studies. *Critical studies in mass communication*, 12(2), 214–39.

Zerubavel, E. (2003). *Time maps: Collective memory and the social shape of the past*. Chicago, IL: University of Chicago Press.

2 From Gardens to Gloom, Toward Grandeur

Over the past 100 years, Hollywood Forever Cemetery has been transformed from a site of austere glamour to a public embarrassment, and recently, into a hip hangout. Throughout these shifting cultural roles, however, the cemetery has remained just that: a place where loved ones—from Hollywood celebrities and politicians to everyday Angelenos—are laid to rest, remembered, and, at times, forgotten. This chapter provides a historical context for a discussion of cemeteries as sites of commemoration, of leisure activities, and as tourist attractions. A brief history of Hollywood Forever expands to look at other notable cemeteries that are sites of cultural memory, along with a discussion of the cultural life of death.

Hollywood Memorial Park (now Hollywood Forever Cemetery) was founded in 1899, a time when the fledgling town of Hollywood had only 500 residents. The cemetery served the city before the entertainment industry transformed it—in 1920, the cemetery sold forty acres of land to Paramount Studios, and today the Paramount backlot is adjacent to Hollywood Forever. Early studio stars and executives are buried at the cemetery, and just as the Paramount water tower can be seen from the cemetery, so are the cemetery grounds visible from the studio lot. Paramount's familiar corporate logo, which adorns the tower, is comprised of a mountain surrounded by a halo of twenty-two stars, representing the studio's original leading actors, including silent film legend Douglas Fairbanks. Buried along with his son, Douglas Fairbanks, Jr., his is one of the most prominent gravesites at Hollywood Forever. Fairbanks Lawn recalls the National Mall, with the sarcophagus set in a marble arch at the end of a long, narrow reflecting pool. The monuments and landscaping of the cemetery make it both aesthetically and culturally appealing. Many of the celebrities interred at Hollywood Forever are found in mausoleum crypts or have flat grass markers at their gravesites, while others have upright tombstones on the grounds. Among the most-visited monuments is a statue of Johnny Ramone, guitar in hand, playing the Ramones' unique, straightforward punk rock into eternity. Visitors to the cemetery pose for photographs beside the memorial and leave behind flowers and notes, which are removed daily by cemetery staff. Although Ramone was cremated after his death from prostate cancer in 2004, he had the cenotaph designed as a place for his fans to remember him. The gravesite of bandmate Dee Dee Ramone, who died of a heroin overdose in 2002, is nearby. This pseudonym is etched into his gravestone, along with his given name, Douglas Glenn Colvin. When the band formed in 1973, all of the members adopted Ramone as a stage name in a show of solidarity and common identity. The grave marker also includes an epitaph: "OK . . . I gotta go now." Hollywood Forever's willingness to allow a comical statement such as this typifies attitudes embraced by the cemetery. While not directly paying homage to actress Joan Hackett, who is buried in Hollywood Forever's Abbey of the Psalms, Ramone's epitaph recalls Hackett's: "Go Away—I'm Asleep."

Johnny Ramone's choice of Hollywood Forever as the site for his memorial indicates the gains the cemetery made in reestablishing its cultural capital. Since Ramone's remains aren't buried at Hollywood Forever, this memorial could have been placed virtually anywhere—perhaps in New York City, where the band rose to fame. As a permanent marker intended as a commemorative site, Ramone's cenotaph is now a gathering place for fans from all over the world. Similarly, Gilbert Rodman (1996) argues that Graceland gives Elvis Presley's fans "a geographic center that other fan communities lack" (p. 128). Graceland enables an immersive experience for Elvis fans, along with the pleasures of being engaged in a fandom community that is physical and perpetually present. While the Ramones fandom pales in comparison to the adoration bestowed upon Presley, the cenotaph, like Graceland, situates fan culture in a tangible, permanent space. The memorial brings a younger generation of visitors to Hollywood Forever, those who might be unlikely to make a pilgrimage to the graves of the cemetery's many black-and-white era film legends. Ramone's memorial also reflects the significance of the cemetery's transformation from a place once so neglected that dozens of families, including the family of makeup artist Max Factor, had their loved ones disinterred and moved elsewhere.

The history of the cemetery is intimately tied to the somewhat-mysterious history of Jules Roth, who first became affiliated with Hollywood Memorial Park in 1937. Although he was able to hide his past for decades, it came to light in the 1990s that Roth had been convicted of stock fraud in the 1920s and served five years of his prison term at San Quentin before being pardoned. He changed his moniker from Jack Roth to Jules Roth but did not change his habits—he embezzled millions of dollars from the cemetery's endowment fund to support his lavish lifestyle. Meanwhile, with little money devoted to maintenance, the grounds and buildings were ignored. The 1994 Northridge earthquake damaged buildings and tombstones and shattered the stained glass in the mausoleums. None of these were repaired. The reflecting pool in front of the Fairbanks sarcophagus was clogged and overflowing. When Roth died in 1998, the bankrupt cemetery was placed on the auction block. Forever Enterprises, spearheaded by then-27-year-old Tyler Cassity, purchased it for a mere $375,000. The company invested millions of dollars to repair damages and refurbish the buildings and grounds, renaming the cemetery in the process. The renovation of Hollywood Forever is widely praised, yet some skepticism remains about the new name, which has been critiqued for evoking the Disneyfication of the cemetery. As Urry and Larsen (2011) links the Disney theme parks metaphor with an experience economy (p. 54), the critique is somewhat apt. As Hollywood Forever has continued to thrive and regain cultural capital, much of the cemetery's draw for the public is through events intended to create a lasting sense of connection, whether the pleasures of an outdoor movie, a musical performance, or the Día de los Muertos celebration. The success of these events depends in part on what has been called the "death positive" movement. The movement advocates for a change in perspective to accept that death is a natural part of life and to encourage an increasing comfort with discussing the realities of mortality.

The Cultural Life of Death

The death positive movement is affected in part by the aging of the Baby Boomer generation. The death care industry is changing—as Baby Boomers contend with the death of their parents and contemplate their own mortality, cremation is on the rise and traditional burial is subsequently declining. The National Funeral Directors Association (NFDA) reports that in 2015 the number of cremations (48.5 percent) nearly equaled the number of burials (51.5 percent). This trend is expected to continue, with cremation eventually outpacing traditional burial. Several factors come into play in these transitions. An interest in the environment has led some to prefer cremation to the permanent placement of one's body in the ground, taking up space. Cost is also an issue: according to the NFDA (2105), direct cremation costs less than $3,000, where funeral services, excluding the cost of a burial plot, average around $7,200. Some prefer to spend their money sending their loved ones on a trip to scatter their ashes rather than to pay for a casket and burial plot.

Another cost-saving and environmentally prudent practice is green burial, and Tyler Cassity is co-owner of Fernwood Cemetery in Mill Valley, California, one of the first green cemeteries in the United States. Green burial, so-named because of its sound environmental practices, means that burial does not include embalming or any other chemicals. The body is placed in a shroud or other biodegradable material so that the body, over time, naturally decomposes and literally returns to the earth. Traditional grave markers are not permitted; boulders and other naturally occurring markers are used instead.

Thomas Lynch (2000), a funeral director, essayist, and poet, sees the changes in the death care industry in the generation that precedes the Baby Boomers, a generation experiencing longer life spans, earlier retirements, and later-life mobility in an unprecedented manner. He poignantly describes his parents' generation not wanting

> to be a burden to their children. They do not want to be "grounded" to the graves they bought, pre-need, back in the old days when people stayed put. Their ashes are FedExed and parcel-posted and UPSed around the hemisphere day and night in little packages, roughly the weight of a bowling ball, roughly the shape of that first starter home, roughly the size of a coffee can squared. Not nearly the full, life-sized burden of a casket, not nearly the bother or expense.
>
> (pp. 89–90)

As frequently as families move in the United States, subsequent generations are likely to leave the cities and towns in which they grew up. The pre-need purchase of a cemetery plot may mean burial in a city where one's family no longer lives, making it unlikely that one's children will be close by to visit and tend to one's grave. As members of Generation X are attending the funerals of their grandparents, or participating in the rituals to spread their ashes, what are their thoughts on burial? Many of them may not have given a thought to their own mortality, while other GenXers, like Tyler Cassity, were confronted by death when AIDS affected the gay community during the 1980s. Cassity arrived in New York City in 1988 at what he describes as "the apex or the heart of the epidemic." Although he was surrounded by an overwhelming sense of death and dying, Cassity also saw that mournful traditional funerals were being replaced with more joyful events: a party at a nightclub, a poetry reading, a dance performance. He says that when broken, the traditional funeral "was much more powerful. It served a purpose again" (Glass, 2000). These experiences profoundly changed Cassity's personal and professional life, leading him to embrace a focus on celebrating a life well lived rather than mourning a death. For many of Cassity's contemporaries, the AIDS epidemic brought about a new awareness of death, as well as the possibilities for new means of commemoration.

Cassity carried innovative ideas for commemoration to Los Angeles, where he builds on a long history of heritage tourism at Hollywood

Forever. The gravesites of hundreds of celebrities render the cemetery as both a historical site and a tourist attraction. Concluding *The Power of Place*, her study of urban sites of memory in Los Angeles, Dolores Hayden (1997) notes that "any historic place, once protected and interpreted, potentially has the power to serve as a lookout for future generations who are trying to plan the future, having come to terms with the past" (p. 247). Contemplating the past is certainly the only way to learn from it, yet historic tours, like the historic places Hayden refers to, are inevitably an interpretation of the past. The stories any tour guide chooses to tell, as well as the gravesites not included in the cemetery tour, frame a particular history for the visitor. Tourists are not merely passive consumers of information provided to them but take on an interpretive and performative role themselves. Dean MacCannell (1976) argued that an "authentic touristic experience involves not merely connecting a marker [which MacCannell defines as 'a piece of information about a sight'] to a sight, but a participation in a collective ritual, in connecting one's own marker to a sight already marked by others" (p. 137). Having been told a story, the tourist now has her own story to tell.

Cemeteries and Perceptions

For the celebrity cemetery, sense of place develops through the memories accumulated by visitors attending Cinespia, Día de los Muertos, Douglas Fairbanks' birthday party, or myriad other events. Cultural geographer J. B. Jackson (1994) describes a contemporary sense of place as being present in localities that "are cherished because they are embedded in the everyday world around us and easily accessible, but at the same time are distinct from that world." He adds that "a visit to one of them is a small but significant event. We are refreshed and elated each time we are there" (p. 158). For Hollywood Forever, this sense of place is accompanied by a distinct sense of time. The convergence of times at the cemetery can create a kind of timelessness—the eternal time of the dead blends with the slow pace of tourist time and the hectic press of Los Angeles time. The historical appeal of the cemetery adds to the sense of timelessness, allowing visitors to share stories of the successes and scandals of the celebrities buried at Hollywood Forever, resurrecting a past in the present. The unique tempo of mourning time runs alongside this timelessness as the period that is set aside in the aftermath of a death for coping, healing, and reordering one's life in the absence of a loved one. The cemetery regulars who drop in to Hollywood Forever for frequent visits use the cemetery to physically dislocate themselves from the time of everyday life, escaping from immediate routines, concerns, and pressures.

Hollywood Forever is working to alter perceptions of the cemetery and to change the alienated relationship between the living and the dead. Beginning in the early twentieth century, the increasing number of individuals who died in the hospital rather than at home had a profound effect on displacing death from everyday life. The physical removal of the dead from the space of the living renders a psychic and emotional distance from the body of the deceased. When death takes place in the hospital, and the body is carted away for burial, the body can be seen as "other," no longer the loved one himself or herself, but "only" the remains, to be properly handled by the professionals of the death care industry. This growing distance and difference between the living person and his or her dead body creates a social discomfort that extends to the cemetery as the physical space where the dead are buried. Cemeteries themselves were instrumental in creating distance between the living and the dead. As the death care industry moved from a community concern to a competitive business in the twentieth century, cemeteries offered full-service perpetual care packages. Family members no longer needed to visit the cemetery to clean and maintain the gravesite because those concerns could be left to the cemetery custodians.

Today, Hollywood Forever closes the gap between the living and the dead by inviting visitors to use the cemetery as social space—if one can enjoy a picnic and a film, listen to music, or celebrate the lives of Mel Blanc and Tyrone Power in the cemetery, then that place can be associated with more than just grieving. When films are shown at Cinespia, four thousand people gather on and around the Fairbanks Lawn, resting on blankets and reclining on lawn chairs. Is the cemetery at night still frightening in the company of so many people, enjoying a screening of *The Maltese Falcon* or *Chinatown*?

Cemeteries as Sites of Cultural Memory

The gravesite pilgrimage is not an uncommon cultural event. Arlington National Cemetery, for example, claims four million visitors a year, as individuals and families travel to Washington to perform acts of personal and cultural memory. But what do these sojourns accomplish, and why do memorial sites matter? Cemeteries serve both personal and public roles; a visit to the gravesite can be a way of spending time with and caring for the memory of a loved one, or it can be a means of engaging local or national history. A typical afternoon at Hollywood Forever readily includes mourners laying fresh flowers beside a headstone and sightseers snapping photos of celebrity graves.

Visiting sites of cultural memory is a way to set into motion the relationship between the present and the past. The significance of heritage tourism is seen in the upsurge of properties included in the National Register of

Historic Places, an increase from 1,200 in 1968 to more than 90,000 in 2008. Hollywood Forever was added to the Register in 1999, the year after the cemetery's restoration began. Not only the graves but also the historically significant architecture of Hollywood Forever effectively evokes the past, from the turn of the previous century to the recent past. The original Bell Tower, built in 1905, still stands, and the Eliza Otis Memorial Chimes, named in honor of the wife of the *Los Angeles Times* founder, are still operating as well. The historic Masonic Lodge on the property was built in 1931 and originally hosted meetings of the local Freemasons. The Lodge is now a venue for concerts, stand-up comedians, and other performances. With a capacity of 150 seats, the Masonic Lodge offers an intimate setting, adding to the cemetery's cultural capital not only because of its heritage, but also as a well-regarded concert venue.

Built in 1938 to display the remains of those who choose cremation, the cemetery's columbarium is a warm, Spanish-style building with a fountain set in the rotunda. A handful of public figures are among those who are memorialized in the columbarium. Celebrities run the gamut from Elmo Lincoln, the first actor to play Tarzan in 1918's *Tarzan of the Apes*, to Lana Clarkson, the starlet found dead in the home of record producer Phil Spector in 2003. Although two generations separate these actors, both have memorial niches that remind the visitor of their roles in celebrity culture. The traditional, and expected, language for the grave marker is often an indication of familial bonds, such as "loving husband" or "devoted father." Lincoln's grave marker simply reads: "Elmo Lincoln/The First Tarzan/1889–1952." His career is privileged over his personal life.

Where Elmo Lincoln's niche contains only an urn holding his cremains, Lana Clarkson's large niche in the columbarium appears like a fan's memorabilia collection. The sides and back of the niche are covered with leopard-patterned cloth, and a large color photograph of Clarkson in a tank top, grinning broadly at the camera, takes up most of the back wall. A marquee card with Clarkson seductively posed in a short red dress is one of several other photographs included. Family members and fans who visit leave flowers, notes, balloons, and other remembrances. Unlike the outdoor memorial for Johnny Ramone, it appears that most of the remembrances for Clarkson are left beside her niche. The presence of these items, in addition to the niche itself, indicates to the visitor that Clarkson is, quite simply, remembered. More complex, however, is the way in which the visitor makes meaning of the entire assembly of images and texts. Her niche is evocative and, like Lincoln's niche, draws on celebrity to indicate her cultural position in time as well as in terms of cultural capital. Including items that are markers of celebrity in the niche informs visitors of the culturally significant career of the person interred there. For example, a few steps away from

Lana Clarkson's niche is the final resting place of Ann Sheridan, Warner Bros.' "Oomph Girl." Sheridan fan Karen McHale learned that her wishes to have her cremains placed in a columbarium in Los Angeles were not carried out. McHale found the executor of Sheridan's will, located her ashes, and arranged for Hollywood Forever to donate a niche for her in the Columbarium. A framed portrait of Sheridan on the cover of *Time* magazine, a significant sign of her fame, is placed beside the urn containing her ashes. While this seems appropriate to the celebrity cemetery, the lack of restrictions Hollywood Forever imposes on what can be included in a niche is unique among cemeteries and allows those who want to be remembered by more than a name and dates of birth and death to create memorable sites of commemoration. By capturing the attention of visitors, these informative and engaging sites of memory keep the names and roles of these actors in circulation. The visitor to the columbarium can act as a beacon, carrying the stories of these bygone celebrities back into contemporary discourse.

The growing popularity of columbarium niches attests to the change in cultural memory as commemoration moves from official declarations to personal, narrative, and multifaceted memories. The inclusion of objects, photographs, and brief documents in a niche create a sense of a person's life in a complex, rich way that is not available on a gravestone. For example, the ashes of actor David White, who portrayed Larry Tate on the television comedy *Bewitched*, are placed in a niche in the Cathedral Mausoleum's Valentino Shrine. White's niche is also a memorial to his son Jonathan, who was killed in the 1998 terrorist attack on Pan Am Flight 103. David White died two years later, following a massive heart attack. A list of his film and television credits and a bronze bust share the small niche with photographs depicting father and son from the time of Jonathan's childhood to his graduation, to images of both men later in life. Through these artifacts, visitors are able to know David White as more than just the roles he played on television and film.

Cultural memory includes the sinners and the saints, sometimes embodied within a single figure. Griffith Jenkins Griffith, who is buried at Hollywood Forever, is considered a great philanthropist: he gave the city of Los Angeles 3,015 acres of land for Griffith Park, the largest metropolitan park in the nation. He also shot his wife in the face, permanently disfiguring her, and consequently served time for attempted murder. The name Griffith will always be in circulation in Los Angeles, as 10 million people make use of the park each year. Yet it is the dramatic and outrageous stories of Griffith's life that make him, as an individual, interesting. Place names—from Griffith Park to O'Hare Airport to Rockefeller Center—become so strongly associated with a site and its function that the person for whom the place is named can fade into the background. The soaring obelisk that marks

Griffith's grave at Hollywood Forever indicates his social significance, and perhaps his enormous ego, but offers no evidence that during his lifetime he was considered "the most hated man in Los Angeles" (Scott, 2001, p. 40). While Griffith's whole story may not be included in a tour book, it is a favorite anecdote in the repertoire of cemetery enthusiasts.

Situated in the cemetery, and activated by the material evidence of history, Griffith's story exemplifies cultural memory as dialogic. While the physical presence of the memorial site does work to sustain a sense of the past, our understandings of and relationship to the past change over time. The gravesite is fixed and unchanging, and there is no certainty that the story it tells will be the same story told in the future. Engagement with places of memory can lead to a shift in the meaning of past events and individuals—spending time at the cemetery, talking with others about the people buried there, and participating in commemorative events enable the past to be reconsidered and reconstituted in the present.

Celebrity culture also provides a reference point for the details of a particular era. To recall a film or song from one's childhood, or any other particular time in our lives, is to recall ourselves—who we were, what we knew and believed, our worldview in that moment. Peter Finch's crypt is across from Rudolph Valentino's. Despite Finch's long career, he may be best remembered for his role in 1976's *Network*, for which he won a posthumous Academy Award. The rallying cry "I'm madder than hell and I'm not going to take it anymore," readily associated with Finch and Howard Beale, the character he played in *Network*, epitomizes the post-Watergate, pre-cable television moment in which the film was made. Other luminaries buried at Hollywood Forever have careers that outlived them; as stars of classic films, they are routinely resurrected on cable networks like American Movie Classics (AMC) and Turner Classic Movies (TCM). These networks serve as important repositories of cultural memory, and the films that are aired provide certain celebrities with more opportunities to be remembered than are afforded others.

Emulating the Other

Shortly after he purchased the cemetery, Cassity shared his vision for Hollywood Forever in an article in the *New York Times Sunday Magazine*. He said, "I want it to be a cultural center—because it is, and the neighborhood needs one" (Spindler, p. 5). Although at the time of the interview, nearby historic Hollywood Boulevard offered more danger than cultural destinations for visitors, the cemetery serves a much broader audience than the immediate neighborhood. Many of the cemetery's visitors travel from distant points in the greater Los Angeles area to attend and participate in events. Those who grew up in the area and spent time there as children and teenagers continue to see the cemetery as leisure and cultural space, but the cemetery and its reputation suffered in the years leading up to its bankruptcy. In his desire to resurrect Hollywood Forever, Tyler Cassity had a model for a cemetery that serves as a cultural center: Forest Lawn Memorial Park, founded in Glendale in 1917.

Cassity's desire to make Hollywood Forever something more than a burial site for the dead certainly reflects the story of Forest Lawn and its longtime general manager, Hubert Eaton. An innovative force in the death care industry, Eaton brought about dramatic changes by creating the nation's flagship lawn park cemetery in Glendale, just east of Los Angeles proper. Eaton envisioned Forest Lawn as a uniform expanse of serene greenspace, absent of the clutter of standing tombstones. "The Builder's Creed," penned by Eaton and exhibited on a monumental stone edifice at Forest Lawn, lays out his vision:

> I shall try to build at Forest Lawn a great park, devoid of misshapen monuments and other customary signs of earthly death, but filled with towering trees, sweeping lawns, splashing fountains, singing birds, beautiful statuary, cheerful flowers, noble memorial architecture with interiors full of light and color, and redolent of the world's best history and romances. I believe these things educate and uplift a community.

Eaton's rhetoric draws on the tradition of Boston's Mount Auburn and the other rural cemeteries that used it as an example. Like Mount Auburn, Eaton saw Forest Lawn as a place where visitors would not only remember their loved ones but could also engage in an aesthetic experience of art and nature that would educate and enlighten.

To complement the greenspace of Forest Lawn and provide an instructive and often religiously uplifting experience for visitors, Eaton collected and commissioned reproductions of famous works of art. The grandeur of the artworks was intended to replace monumental tombstones and sarcophagi, shifting the aesthetic away from a focus on the dead. Despite the desire to attract visitors for instruction and enlightenment, Forest Lawn Glendale and the other five Forest Lawn cemeteries discourage the use of the cemetery space for purposes other than paying respects to one's loved ones and aesthetically engaging the cemetery's collection of artworks. Photography and picnicking are explicitly prohibited.[1]

Unlike Forest Lawn, Hollywood Forever welcomes picnics and tourists; visitors can purchase a map of celebrity gravesites at the cemetery's flower shop. The map, along with the occasional tours of Hollywood Forever, reifies the celebrity of those buried at the cemetery. If Hollywood Forever sees itself as a tourist attraction, it suffers from the relative lack of contemporary celebrities interred there. While Jules Roth neglected the cemetery's buildings and grounds, Hollywood's elite chose other cemeteries for their final resting places. For Hollywood Forever to be a premier tourist destination, the cemetery must make the gravesites of its stars—many of them somewhat obscure to contemporary audiences—attractive to the visitor as worth seeing. Thus the cemetery must function as a publicist for the dead celebrity. Comparing the celebrity to the cultural hero, Daniel Boorstin (1992) elaborates on the fleeting fame that must be reinforced by the image machine, arguing that the celebrity "is the creature of gossip, of public opinion, of magazines, newspapers, and the ephemeral images of movie and television screen" where heroes are "made by folklore, sacred texts, and history books." As such, the hero gains immortality, whereas the celebrity fades away (p. 63). Boorstin does not take into account the possibility of immortality for celebrities, and there are many who take on iconic status. Clearly Rudolph Valentino, Tyrone Power, and Douglas Fairbanks, among others, continue to draw new fans long after death. As the culture industry continues to promote and profit from celebrities after their deaths through DVDs, CDs, books, and other paraphernalia, so does Hollywood Forever benefit from leveraging its cultural capital. For those who want their own permanent property in Hollywood, a new mausoleum is under construction and cremation niches are available in the Cathedral Mausoleum, the Columbarium, and the Abbey of the Psalms.

If Forest Lawn is Tyler Cassity's model for the cemetery as cultural center, then the model for the cemetery as a tourist attraction must certainly lie elsewhere. Hollywood Forever's own history of tourism offers strong traditions to restore.

Cemetery Tours and Walks: Expanding the Tradition

Historic cemeteries, including Hollywood Forever, have long attracted tourists as well as those on a pilgrimage to see the final resting places of the politicians, military leaders, celebrities, and artists they admire. Many of these sites offer guided tours, as well as maps for visitors to locate the gravesites they seek. Green-Wood Cemetery, founded in 1838 in Brooklyn, was among the first rural cemeteries and also among the first to organize a tour for visitors to note the outstanding vistas and architecture on the grounds. Although not a guided tour, maps with a marked path were available for visitors, who numbered around 60,000 annually during the 1850s (Sloane, 1991, p. 60).

Amateur historian Karie Bible conducts the official Hollywood Forever walking tour, typically dressed to honor the Lady in Black who visited

Rudolph Valentino's grave at Hollywood Forever, secretly left roses, and refused to identify herself for years. Bible also participates in the annual Valentino memorial as a tribute to the Lady in Black. As is the case with any tour guide, Bible's rhetoric determines the tourists' perceptions of the cemetery and what public figures interred there matter most. The strategic choices of what celebrities to include depends in part on how engaging the narrative might be: a film star like Florence Lawrence, although not well known by most cemetery tourists, offers a riveting and tragic story to narrate while standing by her grave. Not only was Lawrence the first star to be listed in the opening credits of a film, she also had an unmarked grave until Roddy McDowall, best known for *Planet of the Apes*, donated a marker for her grave in 1991. Hollywood heritage is a palimpsest that is erased and drawn over as long-dead celebrities are rediscovered, as stars die suddenly, or as they live out their long lives in the limelight or in obscurity.

While Hollywood Forever uses these events to reestablish its cultural capital, other cemeteries continue decades-long traditions that are familiar to their local communities. Atlanta's Oakland Cemetery, a rural cemetery established in 1850 on farmland on the outskirts of the city, is now situated in the city center. Like Hollywood Forever, Oakland provides a quiet respite in downtown Atlanta. The last lot at the cemetery was sold in 1884,[2] so visitors are far less likely to encounter mourners at Oakland than at Hollywood Forever, which is still accepting new interments. Priding itself on its architecture, horticulture, and historical significance, Oakland Cemetery positions itself much like a museum or city park, offering afternoon and evening tours focusing on each of these aspects of the cemetery. Taking on the role of city park, Oakland hosts events throughout the year. Events held at Oakland have included an Easter egg hunt, art installations, a themed history tour called "Malts and Vaults," and a *Gone With the Wind* anniversary tour, since Margaret Mitchell, who authored the book, is interred at Oakland.

The events at Hollywood Forever are somewhat in keeping with the social and cultural functions carried out at Oakland, Green-Wood, and several other cemeteries, albeit with a Hollywood twist. Many who feel comfortable with the presentation of a play or the performance of classical music at a cemetery disapprove of Cinespia: showing films in the cemetery, and projecting them on the mausoleum wall, seems disrespectful toward the dead. In some regard, this disapproval veils a highbrow/lowbrow critique; that "culture" can find its place on sacred ground but popular culture cannot.

Despite some criticism, Cinespia has become a mainstay of Los Angeles summer events. Cemeteries in other parts of the country have emulated the film series with varying degrees of success. Congressional Cemetery in Washington, D.C. hosts Cinematery: Movie Night at the Cemetery. In addition to Shakespeare plays and yoga classes, both of which have also been presented at Hollywood Forever, Laurel Hill Cemetery in Philadelphia organizes Cinema in the Cemetery among its many public events. Screenings have included horror classics *The City of the Dead* and George Romero's *Night of the Living Dead*. Screening horror films at the cemetery has been controversial elsewhere. In Chicago, Bohemian National Cemetery was broadly criticized for showing the horror movie *Sinister* in 2015. Bohemian is also home to a columbarium that resembles Wrigley Field, built by Chicago Cubs fan Dennis Mascari. At the dedication in 2009, Mascari said he was inspired to build a celebratory final resting place after visiting his father's grave and feeling more forlorn than he did before entering the cemetery (Drehs, 2009).

These events increase awareness of cemeteries and help to change perceptions of the cemetery from a gloomy, fearful place to a space that is rich in history, architecture, and natural beauty. As visitors participate in events at cemeteries, they are more likely to return as tourists, particularly because of the strong heritage connections that cemeteries hold. While many cemetery events across the country draw on longstanding traditions and encourage visitation to the cemetery, not everyone is an advocate for cemeteries taking on meaning or intent beyond their fundamental purpose. In his book of essays, *Bodies in Motion and at Rest: On Metaphor and Mortality*, Thomas Lynch (2000) finds fault with the performance of a play at a community cemetery. When family members of those buried in the cemetery complained about the play, the thespian group argued that the performance was a celebration of the lives of the dead. Yet in the town's newspaper, opponents argued the cemetery "is full of fathers and mothers and daughters and sons who have no obligation to educate or entertain or instruct the living. Museums and libraries, art galleries and public parks, serve these purposes. The bodies of the dead make Oak Grove a sacred place" (p. 240). Lynch adds his own concern to that of his neighbors, warning that "the harm, of course, is that once the gate is opened it is hard to close, and lost forever is the sacred and dedicated space that is only a cemetery and needs be nothing more" (p. 242). Lynch maintains a traditional perspective on burial and is unwilling to allow the corruption of what he sees as the sacred space of the cemetery. Yet this is also a perspective on death: that the lives of the dead should be revered, but not celebrated, in the cemetery. For Hollywood Forever, the effort to change the public's relationship to the cemetery means overcoming opposition from within the death care industry as well as encouraging new social practices within the cemetery space.

Performing Dark Tourism and Cemetery Tourism

In their seminal 2000 book *Dark Tourism: The Attraction of Death and Disaster*, John Lennon and Malcolm Foley investigate the growing trend of turning sites of death and disaster into tourist destinations. Defining dark tourism as a postmodern phenomenon in which sites of catastrophe become commodities of spectacle, in part as a mirror of our mediated experience of disaster, Lennon and Foley exclude cemeteries from their definition. Categorizing the touristic visit to the cemetery as a pilgrimage, they remark on a perceived difference between cemeteries and sites of dark tourism, arguing that "gravity and reverence are not always characteristic of death sites/grave sites. Jim Morrison's grave in Père Lachaise in Paris questions the whole Victorian bourgeois cultural view of the cemetery as a place of dignity and mourning. Now tourists rather than mourners visit and undertake cemetery tours" (p. 77). The exploits of fans at Jim Morrison's grave are exceptional rather than routine and are certainly notorious. Lennon and Foley imply an inherent disconnection between the touristic experience and the possibility for reverence and gravity. Yet if the visitor to the cemetery, entering that space as a tourist, feels a connection to the famous individuals buried there, why would the visitor not have a sense of reverence? One need only watch footage of the thousands of visitors, walking in almost funereal procession past Elvis Presley's grave, to see the gravity of the gravesite visit. This performance of mourning reinforces the relationships between the fan and the celebrity and among the fans themselves and acts as a cathartic moment in the fan pilgrimage.

More recent work by tourism scholar Philip Stone describes a spectrum of dark tourism sites that does not limit the field to those associated with traumatic loss and devastation. Stone positions "dark resting places"—cemeteries used to promote historic tourism—and "dark shrines"—temporary sites constructed at or near the location of a tragic death—toward the "darker" end of his spectrum. Dark tourism in Hollywood mingles these two categories by including both cemeteries and death sites among its destinations. As the final resting place of many celebrities, Hollywood Forever draws the interest of visitors who are intent on remembering people they did not know but feel connected to through their stardom. Like a site of tragedy, the celebrity cemetery enables a sense of proximity for the visitor who can get closer to the famous person, if only by virtue of his or her material remains.

The touristic visit or pilgrimage to the cemetery can be, like the visit to a sanctioned memorial, a means of stitching oneself into the cultural past. Spending time at a historic site, contemplating its landscape, and listening to its stories can be a powerful means of determining one's place in relation to the past. The experience of significant events, from natural disasters to artistic performances, is increasingly mediated. Although audiences remain at a physical distance from these events, they have emotional affect and social relevance and help shape one's sense of the world. The need to get closer, to see, to touch, and to hear what is known only through mediated experiences, draws visitors to the sites of events experienced virtually.

This sense of presence carries over to the cemetery as well. Regardless of the commemorative acts one might perform to mark the anniversary of the death or birthday of a loved one, or even a beloved celebrity, there is no substitute for being present at that person's grave.[3] At sites of tragic events, many visitors experience a sense of connection by leaving remembrances or participating in other acts of commemoration. At Hollywood Forever, the centuries-old tradition of leaving flowers at a gravesite is expanded to include a variety of material markers and acts of commemoration that are addressed in this book.

The expectations for decorum as a cemetery tourist are likely different from performing the role of tourist in other locales—tourist performance is highly contextualized. For visitors at Hollywood Forever who take Bible's walking tour, expectations are provided at the beginning of the tour with regard to the use of electronic devices, to taking photographs, and to being gracious when encountering mourners. Being a tourist in an operating cemetery entails the possibility of encountering a funeral party, or a mourning spouse or relative who comes to clean the gravesite, leave remembrances, and spend time with the dead. As an increasingly diverse and secular culture changes established relationships with the dead, it is more difficult to know what proper behavior might be in the presence of a mourner who is not a tourist and whose presence in the cemetery is marked by a different set of intentions. At Hollywood Forever, the inclusion of artistic grave markers helps to create a more open environment, but the visitor who knows that the cemetery hosts movies, concerts, yoga classes, and celebrations may have trouble negotiating the appropriate demeanor for a visit to the cemetery. At any tourist destination, visitors learn how to behave from observing others and adjusting to meet specific social norms. Many sites welcome tourists to use smartphones and tablets to access location-appropriate information, especially sites like Arlington National Cemetery that offer online apps to locate specific gravesites. With 624 acres, Arlington requires some mapping for visitors. Talking on the phone, however, would be frowned upon.

Bible's walking tour of Hollywood Forever is offered only every other week. Tourists at the cemetery can opt to purchase a map from the flower shop with celebrity gravesites marked on it, or they may have gathered information from a handful of websites that feature locations of burials at several Los Angeles cemeteries. Those who have been called "post-tourists" will resist the official discourse of the cemetery and its literature, bringing a more cynical and playful attitude to their tourist visit. Yet an argument could easily be made to support the idea that Hollywood Forever is, by design, a post-tourist destination. If tourists determine their behavior by those who surround them, there is certainly a liberating message in watching Bill Obrock, Hollywood Forever's executive vice president, rollerblade around the cemetery in the 2000 HBO documentary *The Young and the Dead.* The desire to replace solemnity with celebration, within the confines of respectable behavior, is at the root of the attitude Hollywood Forever projects.

At the same time, many visitors—especially those passing through the gates of Hollywood Forever for the first time—still struggle with their discomfort being in a cemetery. Along with the post-tourists are the traditional visitors who believe that any cemetery is a site of sacred ground. For those who are willing to find themselves welcomed in the cemetery, a powerful sense of place can develop. The cemetery can facilitate this change, yet each individual must be willing to set aside his or her sense of foreboding and pass through the gates to engage the cemetery as social space. The multiplicity of meanings attached to Hollywood Forever is not unique to cemeteries, nor is it unique to public spaces in general. As a site of both personal memory and cultural memory, Hollywood Forever gives visitors different reasons for coming: some to mourn, some to commemorate, and some as a pilgrimage. At the celebrity cemetery, these meanings can overlap, not only as tourists walk discreetly past mourners, but also as each visitor intent on paying respects to an admired celebrity has his own personal reasons for doing so.

Notes

1 On the reverse side of the map distributed at the front gate and flower shop at Forest Lawn are official guidelines for the visitor. While a color brochure encourages guests to “see the world’s greatest art” at Forest Lawn, the guidelines indicate, contradictorily, that loitering is prohibited: “Persons other than property owners and relatives and friends of deceased persons interred or to be interred in the Forest Lawn Memorial-Parks should not linger or ‘hang around’ on the grounds or in the buildings.” The traditional act of picnicking on cemetery grounds is also explicitly prohibited, as is photography “except at funerals, weddings, and other private services with the consent of the person(s) in charge.” For those with an interest in visiting celebrity gravesites, Forest Lawn’s guidelines translate into a strong prohibition.

2 Although the last lot at Oakland was sold more than a hundred years ago, there are recent interments of note: former Atlanta mayor Maynard Jackson was buried at Oakland in 2003, one of twenty-five mayors interred there. Famed golfer Bobby Jones, an Atlanta native, was buried in 1971. Margaret Mitchell, author of *Gone With the Wind*, was buried at Oakland following her death in 1949.

3 For example, Tracy Terhune, author of *Valentino Forever: The History of the Valentino Memorial Services* and moderator of the “We Never Forget” Rudolph Valentino Facebook page, posted a message to the group announcing that he was taking flowers to Valentino’s grave on the anniversary of the actor’s birthday. Several group members responded, expressing both their appreciation and the wish that they, too, could be in Los Angeles to commemorate Valentino’s birthday in person.

References

Drehs, W. (2009, April 23). For some fans, Cubs are an undying love. *ESPN.com*. Retrieved from www.espn.com/chicago/columns/story?id=4090319&columnist=drehs_wayne

Glass, I. (Director). (2000, December 29). Kodak Moments of the Dead [*This American life*]. Chicago, IL: WBEZ for National Public Radio.

Hayden, D. (1997). *The power of place: Urban landscapes as public history*. Cambridge, MA: MIT Press.

Jackson, J. B. (1994). *A sense of place, a sense of time*. New Haven, CT: Yale University Press.

Lynch, T. (2000). *Bodies in motion and at rest: On metaphor and mortality*. New York, NY: W. W. Norton & Co.

MacCannell, Dean. (1976). *The tourist: A new theory of the leisure class*. New York, NY: Schocken Books.

National Funeral Directors Association. (2015). *Statistics*. Retrieved from www.nfda.org/news/statistics

Rodman, G. B. (1996). *Elvis after Elvis: The posthumous career of a living legend*. New York, NY: Routledge.

Scott, T. L. (2001). *The stars of Hollywood Forever*. Los Angeles, CA: Tony Scott Publishing.

Sloane, D. C. (1991). *The last great necessity: Cemeteries in American history*. Baltimore, MD: Johns Hopkins University Press.

Urry, J. and Larsen, J. (2011). *The Tourist Gaze 3.0*. Los Angeles, CA: Sage.

3 The Celebrity Cemetery

Hollywood Forever's significance as a site of public memory has long been tied to silent film star Rudolph Valentino and the annual memorial service for the actor, ongoing since his interment in 1926. With this rich past, Hollywood Forever maintained cultural currency even as the grounds were neglected, the perpetual care fund drained by embezzlement, and the front gate finally padlocked in the 1990s. Renovation and promotion as a tourist attraction led the cemetery to once again become a significant cultural site. The presence of celebrity gravesites shapes Hollywood Forever as social space in which mourners, fans, and tourists intermingle. Through memorial celebrations and commemorative events for stars such as Douglas Fairbanks and Johnny Ramone, Hollywood Forever becomes a site where fans gather and return, taking photographs and leaving remembrances to demonstrate their ongoing involvement with the celebrities they admire. The actors, directors, and musicians interred at Hollywood Forever are deployed as figures of cultural memory when meaning-making about the past is attached to their lives and creative work. This chapter considers specific instances of celebrities interred at Hollywood Forever that demonstrate the close connection between stars and fandoms.

In his comprehensive study *Understanding Fandom*, Mark Duffett (2013) offers a straightforward yet broad definition of media fandom as "the recognition of a positive, personal, relatively deep, emotional connection with a mediated element of popular culture" (p. 2). That Duffett specifies the positive aspects of the connection between fan and celebrity deliberately undoes preconceptions that fans are always obsessive and pathological in their admiration. Certainly most audience members experience pleasure at some time with media texts they enjoy, and this could be understood as the formative setting for fandom. As early as 1956, Donald Horton and Richard Wohl identified and named parasocial relationships as the one-way relationships between actors and audiences in which audience members felt an attachment to particular actors or the characters they portray. In a hypermediated culture like most of the United States in the twenty-first century, parasocial relationships are normalized to the point that they are taken for granted. That sports fans talk about "their team" and athletes as if they are familiar friends does not necessarily register as an important fandom. Thanks to social media and the internet, contemporary celebrities populate our lives every day. Because the filter of publicists is no longer present, and fans can function like paparazzi, taking photos of celebrities and relating stories for broad audiences via the internet, the access to celebrities and their lives feels familiar for audiences. These two paths to familiarity—parasocial relationships and identification—enable fans to create lasting bonds with celebrities.

Normalizing fandom plays out in the instance of celebrity deaths; while it is routine to post announcements and commemorations on social media when a celebrity dies, there are threads of disaffection with these posts. Fans feel a sense of loss. They have a desire to grieve because grief is a way to give voice to pain. Yet there are broad critiques of those who are overly emotional in their expression of sadness when a celebrity dies. Many believe that the open lamenting for the death of a person you did not know personally is inappropriate and crosses a line of decency.

As is evident in the following narratives regarding Florence Lawrence and Rudolph Valentino, the parasocial relationships between fans and celebrities are often constructed through the mechanisms of publicists and the news and entertainment media.

The Celebrity Cemetery

The name Florence Lawrence is not widely known, and was not known at all at the beginning of her Hollywood career. Yet Lawrence, who was buried in an unmarked grave at Hollywood Memorial Park in 1938, marks the beginning of the star system and celebrity culture as we know it. Actor Roddy McDowall, who was a collector of celebrity memorabilia, gave her a grave marker in 1991, and Carl Laemmle gave her a name in 1910. In cinema's early years, actors were not credited by name and Lawrence, who had signed to Biograph with director D.W. Griffith, became known as "The Biograph Girl." She was hired away by Laemmle, who gave her individual billing, making Lawrence the first star to be known to the public by name. Yet Laemmle wanted to ensure that her name would be familiar to movie-going audiences. In what is widely considered the first celebrity publicity stunt, Laemmle planted a story that Lawrence had died suddenly. Soon after, he retracted the story, and Lawrence made an appearance in St. Louis, well received by an adoring crowd that may not have given her much thought before their vicarious emotional involvement in her fabricated death and resurrection.

Photographs and brief biographies of Lawrence appear in many of the books and websites for tourists with an interest in celebrity burials. While some of these texts are indicative of capitalizing on interest in celebrity culture, even after celebrities are dead, the authors of several books and websites are cemetery hobbyists themselves. Jim Tipton, founder of the Find a Grave website, created the repository of cemetery information in 1995 when he was unable to find an online resource that addressed his interest in celebrity gravesites. Thousands of cemetery hobbyists have contributed images and text to the site, which now features more than 20,000 famous individuals. The 400,000 registered users at *Findagrave.com* indicate the broad popularity of and interest in celebrity graving, as well as the significance of cemeteries as a site of cultural heritage.

The presence of celebrity gravesites shapes Hollywood Forever as social space in which mourners, fans, and tourists intermingle. In organized tours and as casual visitors, people learn about and engage with the history of celebrity culture as they stroll through the cemetery. Memorial services and commemorative events at Hollywood Forever and other Los Angeles area cemeteries show how these spaces become sites where fans gather and return, taking photographs and leaving remembrances to demonstrate their ongoing involvement with the celebrities they continue to admire. Rudolph Valentino, who was interred in a mausoleum niche at Hollywood Forever owned by screenwriter June Mathis, is an excellent example of the rich afterlife of a celebrity burial. Although Mathis offered the niche as a temporary burial site after Valentino's sudden death, he remains in the same location, with June Mathis now buried beside him. Valentino's life, death, and afterlife offer a lens through which the history of Hollywood Forever and its relationship to celebrity culture can be examined. The mysterious mourner known as the Lady in Black, and the women who fought for the status and notoriety associated with the role, tells a story of fandom that demonstrates the enduring cultural significance of celebrities long after their death. Spanning more than ninety years, the Valentino memorial services trace the history of Hollywood Forever from prominence through decay to resurrection.

"We Never Forget"[1]

Through his dazzling performance of the Argentine tango, Rudolph Valentino created a seductive image in New York clubs, on tour, and on screen. His expertise as a dancer, along with his penetrating gaze, turned him into an international sex symbol and earned him the nickname "the Great Lover."[2] The young Italian film star was catapulted into the spotlight in part because he was marked as an exotic Other, one who carried an air of sexuality and mystery because of his difference. The release of *The Sheik* in

1921 solidified Valentino's stardom, making him a focus of news and gossip across the world.

Valentino was in New York City in August 1926 on a promotional tour for *The Son of the Sheik* and fell ill after a party at the home of a friend. Following emergency surgery for appendicitis and gastric ulcers, newspapers and radio kept a close watch on Valentino's failing health. Crowds gathered outside Polyclinic Hospital and others called for updates on his condition; with as many as eight to ten calls coming in every minute, extra operators were brought in to handle the volume ("Valentino Sinking"). Valentino died on August 23, at the age of 31. Campbell's Funeral Home offered its services gratis, in an act of benevolence mingled with capitalizing on celebrity death. Frank Campbell made clear, however, that he would not be unhappy should United Artists, with whom Valentino was under contract, offer compensation. Thousands of New Yorkers—some devoted fans, some curiosity seekers—lined up to wait for the opportunity to view Valentino in repose. More than 9,000 people each hour passed through the funeral home, with an estimated 100,000 visitors over three days. Paying one's respects to a prominent statesman or celebrity allows the individual to experience a sense of belonging by joining with others in a meaningful moment in popular culture. Cultural capital is also gained through being able to convey to others the experience of having "been there."

The Son of the Sheik was yet to have its full nationwide theatrical release, and the studio faced a potentially devastating financial loss. Valentino biographer Irving Shulman (1967) points out that in the 1920s "moving pictures starring dead actors and actresses played to empty theaters. The superstitious public apparently believed it indecent to watch dead people perform in their full vigor" (pp. 3–4). Yet public demand for *The Son of the Sheik* was surprisingly strong. Millions flocked to the theaters to see Valentino in his final performance. Fans and onlookers numbering in the thousands lined the streets of Los Angeles on September 14, 1926 to watch the funeral procession as Rudolph Valentino's body was transported from the Church of the Good Shepherd in Beverly Hills to Hollywood Memorial Park. Admission to witness Valentino's interment in the Cathedral Mausoleum was by invitation only, yet the annual memorial services at the cemetery have always been open to the public.

The Valentino memorial service is the longest-running annual event in Los Angeles, other than the Easter Sunrise Service at the Hollywood Bowl, which began in 1921. With this rich history, the memorial becomes more than a remembrance of a particular film star. It is transformed into a cultural event, specifically a Hollywood event. The cemetery did not organize the Valentino memorial service until 1951; for twenty-five years prior, the commemorative acts of fans occurred spontaneously. Yet due to the popular culture phenomenon of the Lady in Black, the anniversary of Valentino's death routinely received news coverage and public interest. When Forever Enterprises took ownership of the cemetery in 1998, they also took over the Valentino memorial services, adding a video montage to the service and an evening screening of a Valentino film with live accompaniment.

The cultural memory of a particular site can blend with personal memory through one's experiences of that place over time. Cultural critic Lucy Lippard (1998) argues that we can transform a space into place, and develop our own sense of place, by listening to its stories and making those stories our own. "Narratives articulate relationships between teller and told, here and there, past and present. In the absence of shared past experience, in a multicentered society, storytelling . . . take[s] on a heightened intensity" (p. 50). The Valentino memorial services engage this influential means of connection: in the early years, many of the speakers recalled their encounters with Valentino; since most of those who knew Valentino have died, now historians and friends retell their stories as part of the memorial program. Musical tributes and video presentations are also part of the annual gathering that usually fills the Cathedral Mausoleum where Valentino is interred.

Although Hollywood Forever designated amateur historian Karie Bible as the official Lady in Black at the 2002 Valentino memorial service, women still come to the services dressed in vintage black dresses and veils, both in homage to Valentino and to carry on the tradition themselves. The persistent performance of the Lady in Black can be read through the lens of camp. Referring to the revitalized interest in classic Hollywood films *What Ever Happened to Baby Jane?* and *Sunset Boulevard*, cultural critic Andrew Ross (2002) sees camp as an instance in which "the products (stars, in this case) of a much earlier mode of production, which has lost its power to produce and dominate cultural meanings, become available in the present, for redefinition according to contemporary codes of taste" (p. 312). Ross' perspective is fitting for Valentino as well, as one of the pleasures in Valentino fandom is in recovering a Hollywood figure who is occasionally referred to in today's popular culture but whose work—along with most silent films—is more broadly thought of in archival terms than as useful and relevant entertainment.

Among Valentino fans, a pop culture icon is elevated to a level of reverence, in part through a celebration of the antiquated conventions of silent film. Many who attend the memorial services also collect celebrity memorabilia, with some interested exclusively in items owned by or relating to Valentino. Camp is part of collecting as well, as the purchase—often at auction—and display of memorabilia aestheticizes everyday objects and elevates them to a level of preciousness. Valuable items such as Valentino's hairbrush, glassware, and ashtrays, as well as invitations to the funerals in New York and Beverly Hills, have been displayed in glass cases at the annual memorial service. For the more casual (although perhaps not less devoted) collector, lobby cards, photographs, posters, and vintage commercial items bearing the star's image or signature are the usual fare. Unlike Valentino's personal effects, these items are valued by collectors in part because of their relative rarity but also because they are material markers that translate fandom into the object world.

Hollywood Forever can be, in fact, a fitting moniker for the place where the physical remains of hundreds of celebrities are placed in perpetuity. There is always the possibility, however remote, that Angelica Huston will visit the gravesite of her father, director John Huston, or Smiths frontman Morrissey will stroll the cemetery grounds looking for the ideal location for his gravesite.[3] The trace of celebrity is ever present: the informed visitor to Hollywood Forever is aware of those who have passed through before to take part in funerals or to pay their respects, from Bing Crosby serving as an honorary pallbearer for Marion Davies to Charlie Chaplin, laying his mother to rest. As Valentino's gravesite was long considered a must-see stop for those new to Hollywood, and especially those seeking stardom themselves, celebrities including Jean Harlow, James Dean, Frank Sinatra, and Sammy Davis, Jr. are reported to have visited the cemetery.[4] The desire to occupy the same space where others have once stood at the cemetery is similar to the tourist experience at the Chinese Theatre, standing in the footsteps of beloved celebrities. The power of place, common among Hollywood Forever, the Chinese Theatre, and countless historical sites, draws tourists to experience the past through situated presence.

Celebrity, Situated

A typical Sunday afternoon at Hollywood Forever resembles Sunday at most cemeteries—mourners file out of the chapel following an early funeral and walk in slow, small groups to their cars. Being the weekend, visitors come throughout the day to remember their loved ones and to tend to their graves. Some clear away old, wilted flowers and replace them with fresh ones; others burn ceremonial incense; and some simply sit in contemplative silence or utter a few quiet prayers. At Hollywood Forever, things are slightly different. In addition to the funeral services and the tending of graves underway, small clusters of visitors gather in the back of the cemetery, seeking the burial places of the famous. Tourists with cameras and smartphones in hand traverse the Garden of Legends, where they locate and photograph the final resting places of Cecil B. DeMille, Janet Gaynor, and Nelson Eddy, among others. Fans of more contemporary celebrities may seek out the gravesites of Mickey Rooney or Don Adams. The doors of the Cathedral Mausoleum are propped open, as visitors pay their respects to Rudolph Valentino, Peter Lorre, or Barbara La Marr. The buzz of human activity is not solemn, but neither is it disrespectful. The social scripts for mourning in a cemetery are carried to Hollywood Forever and dictate the behavior of visitors, although with an upbeat edge. This is appropriate for the cemetery intent on celebrating life rather than mourning death.

Hollywood Forever is not the only cemetery in Los Angeles to host memorial services in honor of its famous permanent residents. Hillside Memorial Park holds events to honor Al Jolson and Jack Benny, two of the best-known Hollywood legends interred there. Both have sumptuous burial sites: Benny and his wife Mary are interred in an enormous black marble sarcophagus in the Hall of Graciousness in Hillside's mausoleum. Jolson's memorial, complete with a 120-foot waterfall and towering pillars, is visible to passing traffic on the nearby 405 Freeway. A memorial salute to Jolson at Hillside Memorial Park included remarks from members of the Jolson Society along with a wreath-laying and a color guard from the Jewish War Veterans. Rather than marking the anniversary of his death, the International Jack Benny Fan Club hosts an annual service at Hillside as part of a day-long celebration held on his birthday. Like Hillside, tiny Westwood Village Memorial Park hosts an annual service for its most famous resident, Marilyn Monroe, who died in 1962. Monroe's grave is one of the most visited celebrity burial sites in the world, with an estimated 350 people coming to pay tribute each day (Masek, 2001, p. 187). Visitors are welcome to sit and reminisce on a white stone bench donated by two Marilyn Monroe fan clubs to mark the thirtieth anniversary of her death.

If dying can be thought of as a liminal space between life and death, then in celebrity culture there is another liminality between death and burial, an in-between time during which the public may take stock of an individual's cultural contributions to consider his or her place in cultural memory. When death occurs suddenly and unexpectedly, the public experiences a heightened sense of loss, as in the deaths of Prince, John Lennon, and Rudolph Valentino, among others. When Douglas Fairbanks, Jr. died in New York in 2000, his heirs debated whether burial with his father at Hollywood Forever would be appropriate. Less than two years had passed since the cemetery was purchased by Forever Enterprises, and prior to the takeover the family considered disinterring Douglas Fairbanks, Sr. because of the deplorable conditions at the cemetery. Fairbanks Jr.'s burial at Hollywood Forever marked a turning point for reasserting both its reputation and the confidence of the celebrity community. Regarding the Fairbanks funeral, Tyler Cassity says, "It was very dramatic. He was a knight, so there was a representative from the queen. There was a full honor guard, 21-gun salute, but it was beautiful to see this whole area come alive again with a service and for the cemetery to have this old tradition kind of renewed" (Montagne). With the moss cleaned from the reflecting pool, the overgrown weeds cleared, and renovation underway, Hollywood Forever's revival was in full bloom as family, fans, and media gathered to pay their last respects to Douglas Fairbanks, Jr.

Subculture Celebrity

Henry Jenkins (2006), one of the founding theorists of fandom studies and participatory culture, recognizes the important role that fandom can play in creating identity and belonging in marginalized communities. He writes that fandom is "a vehicle for marginalized subcultural groups (women, the young, gays, and so on) to pry open spaces for their cultural concerns within dominant representations; fandom is a way of appropriating media texts and rereading them in a fashion that serves different interests" (p. 64). Cultural expression of subcultures often involves not only reading against hegemonic norms, but also performing subculture in conjunction with the style of celebrities with whom they identify. Hollywood Forever has been the choice for many artists and performers whose gravesites express their personal style. The cemetery's lack of restrictions on graves and niches and openness to creative expression has made it the choice for burial for marginalized celebrities and their fans.

While casual tourists have a general appreciation for the historic and aesthetic aspects of Hollywood Forever, they lack the enchantment of the fans and cemetery hobbyists who enthusiastically seek out particular graves, taking photographs and often leaving flowers, notes and other remembrances.[5] Fans of cartoon voice master Mel Blanc, for example, leave Daffy Duck and Bugs Bunny figures at his grave, which is marked with the appropriate and humorous epitaph, "That's all folks." Leaving a stuffed animal at a gravesite indicates planning and intention, and the remembrance is a performance of fandom. Not only does the fan leave a gift for the person he or she admires, which is itself a communicative act, but the presence of items left by others indicates to visitors that the person interred there is honored and remembered. Such remembrances may, in fact, draw the attention of other visitors. For example, the candles, gold stars, drumsticks, cigarettes, and flower petals artfully arranged on punk rocker Bianca Halstead's gravestone, a few steps away from Dee Dee Ramone's, create a visual panorama that invites curiosity and closer examination.

Leaving remembrances is a performance of the emotional attachments that are at the heart of fandom. These attachments are articulated in a variety of ways: as consumer, as producer of information, as community members, and as tourists. Making a pilgrimage to a celebrity gravesite is often considered a significant milestone in fandom. The thousands who visit Elvis Presley's grave at Graceland or venture to Père Lachaise Cemetery in Paris to pay tribute to Jim Morrison offer strong examples. In some instances, fans take a larger role by funding the burial of a celebrity, as is the case of Maila Nurmi, best known as Vampira, the television horror movie hostess character she created in the 1950s. Vampira was the predecessor of the 1980s horror host Elvira, whose persona owes a great deal to Nurmi. In his book about Nurmi, Scott Poole (2014) poignantly describes her burial site: "An etched image of one of her most famous TV images appears on the headstone. A web stretches behind her, strange and complex like the web of her life, while she stands as she was in 1954, morbidly shaped and alien, the original vampire lady. 'Hollywood Legend,' the stone lies" (p. 220).

Vampira was also a character in the cult classic *Plan 9 from Outer Space*. Nurmi's costar in the film, Paul Marco, is also buried at Hollywood Forever. Marco's gravestone is marked "Kelton the Cop Forever," reflecting the role he played in *Plan 9* and two other Ed Wood films. For those who were close to the reclusive Nurmi late in her life, Hollywood Forever was the right choice for her burial. Not only is she buried in a cemetery that celebrates stardom in all of its facets, but she is also interred in a place where cult film fans are more likely to pay tribute to her.

Holly Woodlawn, the transgender star of Andy Warhol's Factory, also died in 2015. She was the inspiration for Lou Reed's song "Take a Walk on the Wild Side" and filmed appearances in two episodes of the television series *Transparent* shortly before her death. Her niche features a glamorous photo accompanying her name and dates of birth and death. In the midst of a cemetery that welcomes complex, highly decorated burial sites, the stark simplicity of Woodlawn's gravesite speaks to a certain kind of elegance.

Among the unusual burial services at Hollywood Forever is one organized by Rick Rubin, who has a long history with the cemetery. Rubin co-founded Def Jam Records with Russell Simmons in 1984. When he discovered the word "def" was one of the new words scheduled for inclusion in the 1993 edition of Webster's dictionary, Rubin bought a burial plot at Hollywood Memorial Park and organized a funeral for "def." Rev. Al Sharpton presided and delivered the eulogy, explaining the rationale for the funeral by asserting that def meant "more than excellent. Like, def-iantly excellent with a bang. Now the bang is out of def. It has lost its exclusivity to the in def-iant crowd. It died of terminal acceptance" (Keister, 2004, p. 241). Rick Rubin's relationship to the cemetery offers evidence that Hollywood Forever has a long history as a space where the solemnity of funereal practices does not exclude the possibility for the whimsical or lighthearted act of cultural commemoration.

Hollywood Forever has also been the location for more somber funerals. Scott Weiland, former lead singer of the Stone Temple Pilots and Velvet Revolver, died from an accidental overdose while on tour in 2015. Weiland had a long history of drug use and addiction that was part of the celebrity narrative defined for him by the media. As rock 'n' roll culture has become part of Hollywood Forever's aura, due in part to the annual events commemorating Johnny Ramone, the cemetery was a fitting site for Weiland's funeral. Yet as *Billboard* (2016) reported, it is also a site of memory for Weiland and his widow Jamie, who often watched movies at Cinespia. Although Weiland was cremated and his ashes were not interred at the cemetery, many news outlets and fans mistakenly reported that he was buried at Hollywood Forever. One reason for this misinformation was the caption for an Instagram photo posted by Chris Kushner, wife of Weiland's former bandmate, Dave Kushner: "A very sad day when u bury a friend. He was a good man" (Buchanan, 2016).

In the weeks following Scott Weiland's death, fans made a pilgrimage to Hollywood Forever to pay tribute to the singer. A fan who visited the cemetery posted a message on a Stone Temple Pilots fan website, noting that the security guard said that at least ten people a day visited the cemetery looking for Weiland's gravesite. It is not surprising that despite not having her original intentions fulfilled, Hollywood Forever still had appeal for a rock fan: "I did however see Bugsy Siegel and Johnny Ramon [sic]. It's a beautiful place, but Scott isn't there. Just in case anyone is planning on going . . ." (Buchanan, 2016).

Weiland's family chose to have a small private ceremony at Hollywood Forever. When singer and songwriter Chris Cornell committed suicide in May 2017, his family organized a funeral service that included visitation and performances by friends and fellow rock musicians. Cornell's ashes where interred beside the cenotaph honoring Johnny Ramone, as the two were friends. Following the service, fans and visitors were invited to visit Cornell's gravesite at Hollywood Forever. Hundreds of fans paid their respects and left flowers, notes, and other remembrances. Like Rudolph Valentino's death more than eighty years prior, the cemetery welcomed fans to come together and commemorate a star whose cultural contributions were held dear by fans. In late 2017, Chris Cornell's brother Peter wrote in an open letter to fans that he visits Chris' grave at Hollywood Forever every week: "I talk to him. And I cry. We brought him flowers and organized the flowers, notes, candles, medallions and photos that people from all over the world bring to him" (Buchanan, 2017). By creating a space for fans to remember Cornell, the cemetery also enables communication between his fans and his family.

The practices of tourists and fans at the cemetery demonstrate the significance of celebrity culture, showing how people use their relationships to celebrities as sites of identity formation and expression. The flowers and remembrances they leave behind draw the interest of other visitors and are material evidence that a particular celebrity is remembered and commemorated. Hollywood Forever welcomes fans to organize events in honor of stars from Douglas Fairbanks and Tyrone Power to Bianca Halstead and Johnny Ramone. These events temporarily transform the cemetery into a space of celebration. Using the cemetery as social space raises questions about protocol: if these are unconventional practices, what are the guidelines for appropriate behavior? How should tourists and visitors behave in the company of mourners? Who decides what constitutes "respect" for the living and the dead? Such questions come to bear significantly at Cinespia, when as many as 4,000 visitors gather to enjoy a picnic dinner and a film in the open, outdoor space of the Fairbanks Lawn.

Notes

1 In 1928, at the second annual memorial service for Rudolph Valentino, an enormous floral display in the shape of a cross was emblazoned with the phrase "We never forget." Many Valentino devotees have taken this phrase to be their personal mission, collecting memorabilia, participating in and promoting silent film festivals, and paying tribute to Valentino at Hollywood Forever.

2 For extensive treatments of Rudolph Valentino's life, see Emily Leider's *Dark Lover: The Life and Death of Rudolph Valentino* (New York: Farrar, Straus and Geroux, 2003) and Irving Shulman's 1967 biography, *Valentino* (New York: Trident Press, 1967). Both Leider and Shulman address Valentino's death and its aftermath, which is covered in extensive detail by Allan Ellenberger in *The Valentino Mystique: The Death and Afterlife of the Silent Film Idol* (Jefferson, NC: McFarland and Company, 2005).

3 Morrissey announced his wishes to be buried at Hollywood Forever in a 2007 article in British music magazine NME. See www.nme.com/news/morrissey/28873

4 In the documentary *The Young and the Dead*, Tyler Cassity interviews Bud Testa, longtime organizer of the Rudolph Valentino memorial service. Testa gives Cassity a list of celebrities known to have visited Valentino's grave.

5 Joshua Gamson uses the terms "hobbyist" and "tourist" to distinguish among the attitudes of those who attend events in order to engage in celebrity watching. He notes that "the spectators fall into two detectable groups: hobbyists, ranging from the serious to the casual, and tourists. Both are mixed in terms of age, gender, and race. The hobbyists tend to be more serious about celebrity watching; they are regulars at such events. The activity of the tourists differs from the hobbyists' less in kind as in the degree of its seriousness" (130). These terms readily carry over from watching celebrities arrive at an event to seeking out celebrity gravesites.

References

Buchanan, B. (2016, January 1). Scott Weiland is not buried at Hollywood Forever Cemetery. *Alternative Nation*. Retrieved from www.alternativenation.net/scott-weiland-not-buried-hollywood-forever-cemetary/

Buchanan, B. (2017, September 25). Incredible Chris Cornell family photos released: "We had comfort with each other." *Alternative Nation*. Retrieved from www.alternativenation.net/incredible-chris-cornell-family-photos-released-comfort/

Duffett, M. (2013). *Understanding fandom: An introduction to the study of media fan culture*. New York, NY: Bloomsbury.

Jenkins, H. (2006). *Fans, bloggers, and gamers: Exploring participatory culture*. New York, NY: New York University Press.

Keister, D. (2004). *Stories in stone: A field guide to cemetery symbolism and iconography*. New York, NY: MJF Books.

Lippard, L. (1998). *The lure of the local: Sense of place in a multicentered society*. New York, NY: New Press.

Masek, M. J. (2001). *Hollywood remains to be seen: A guide to the movie stars' final homes*. Nashville, TN: Cumberland House.

Poole, W. S. (2014). *Vampira: Dark goddess of horror*. Berkeley, CA: Soft Skull Press.

Ross, A. (2002). Uses of camp. In F. Cleto (Ed.), *Camp: Queer aesthetics and the performing subject: A reader* (pp. 308–329). Ann Arbor, MI: University of Michigan Press.

Shulman, I. (1967). *Valentino*. New York, NY: Trident Press.

Valentino sinking; Second crisis near; Pleurisy spreads. (1926, August 23). *New York Times*, 1.

4 On the Mausoleum Wall

In the Independent Film Channel/Acura promotional short film *The Projectionists*, four 30-something hipster men drive around Los Angeles debating whether popcorn or chocolate is the ideal movie snack. They drive past a number of buildings, including Frank Gehry's Walt Disney Concert Hall, sizing up and criticizing each one. Their purpose is not clear until the car pulls up in front of a vast green lawn and the young men approvingly eye the long, low wall of a building beyond the grass. The men get out of the car and open its trunk, where a projector is pointed at the wall. A wide shot shows the four men sitting in lawn chairs beside the car, contentedly watching a film projected on the wall. The projectionists are not alone in finding this to be a fine place to screen a film; yet one might need to be familiar with Hollywood Forever to recognize the Fairbanks Lawn as the site for this guerilla drive-in screening. This vast expanse of grass behind the tall, arched sarcophagus of Douglas Fairbanks Sr. and Jr. is broken only by three small family mausoleums. The lawn runs alongside the Cathedral Mausoleum, an ornate Italian Renaissance-inspired building that was the largest mausoleum in the world at the time of its completion. Thanks to Cinespia, that wall has been the screening space for a popular outdoor movie series since 2002.

The first screening on the Fairbanks Lawn was held in conjunction with the 1999 Rudolph Valentino memorial service. Building on decades-long traditions, Hollywood Forever expanded the annual event by screening Valentino's last film, *The Son of the Sheik*, projecting it on the exterior wall of the mausoleum. Chairs arranged on the Fairbanks Lawn provided a comfortable makeshift outdoor theater for Valentino fans (Terhune, 2004, p. 192). Hollywood set designer John Wyatt, who ran a film club called Cinespia, was inspired by the Valentino tribute. When his club grew too large to attend screenings as a group, Wyatt sought a place to show films himself (Epstein, 2005). He approached Tyler Cassity with the idea of screening classic films at Hollywood Forever, and Cinespia launched at the cemetery in 2002. On a typical summer Saturday night, as many as 4,000 Angelenos enjoy picnic dinners, music, and movies on the cemetery grounds. As Matt,[1] a frequent Cinespia moviegoer explains, the experience begins long before he and his friends arrive at the cemetery:

> When I know what's playing, I'll send the e-mail to my friends saying, "This is on." Or someone will send the e-mail out: "This is on at the cemetery, who's in?" We'll start creating a little bit of excitement. And then it actually comes around. We'll figure out who's bringing what food. One of my friends always goes and gets these Vietnamese sandwiches that are spectacular. Everyone generally brings something. It's comparable to a potluck dinner party. Everyone comes over and you're just chilling with your group, with good friends. You're listening to music, during dinner, and not only are you listening to music at the cemetery but you don't have to do anything with the music. There's somebody there who's thinking about it for you, putting on these records, and just wants you to have a good time. We go, we stake out our spot, and we set up our blankets and our chairs and start eating dinner, and drinking a little bit. We try to get there when it opens, at the beginning, because it's just nicer to be done with all that by the time the movie starts.

Matt describes the festive environment created by the comfortable rituals of sharing food with friends and gathering with hundreds of others to listen to music and watch a film. Where Matt and his friends are at ease with spending the evening in a cemetery surrounded by thousands of graves, many find their first visit to Cinespia somewhat ominous. As Hollywood Forever is transformed into social space, however, most visitors easily forget the foreboding aspects of being in a cemetery. Through this transformation, Cinespia can create a powerful sense of place for repeat visitors.

Creating a Sense of Place

Communal public space is one of the benefits of attending Cinespia; entering into a shared space, establishing your spot on the lawn, and getting acquainted with your temporary neighbors, perhaps exchanging food or drinks, happens without any overt plan. Although John Wyatt was merely looking for an interesting space to show classic films, Cinespia now does important cultural work by creating and perpetuating a temporary but recurring public space, what Ray Oldenburg (1999) refers to as a "third place." Beyond home and work, third places are those where individuals feel welcome, comfortable, and at ease. The kind of shared experience found in third places is important to one's quality of life. As the sun sets before a film is shown at Cinespia, the images of both classic and obscure film posters are projected on the mausoleum wall while disc jockeys play music for the crowd. The pre-screening entertainment can create this essential interaction Oldenburg describes. Matt and his friends, as previously noted, appreciate that "there's somebody there who's thinking about it for you, putting on these records, and just wants you to have a good time," like the host of a party who selects the background music for his guests.

Cinespia creates and perpetuates a temporary but recurring public space. A landscape like the Fairbanks Lawn at Hollywood Forever can serve a social function merely by virtue of being space shared among individuals within a community. It is, after all, in public space that people can spend time with others and establish the bonds that form community. J. B. Jackson (1980) argued that landscapes should meaningfully fulfill basic needs for community and belonging: "the need for sharing some of those sensory experiences in a familiar place: popular songs, popular dishes, a special kind of weather supposedly found nowhere else" that enable people to commonly share an event in a unique place (p. 16). He notes that these characteristics allow us to remember a place with an emotional connection. By situating Cinespia on the cemetery grounds, Hollywood Forever becomes a space that can alternatively provide both celebration and solitude. The conjunction of these two things—the social space of summer Saturday nights and the everyday space of quiet and reflection—allows Hollywood Forever to become a distinctively meaningful place for visitors.

Cinespia resurrects social practices of picnicking in the garden landscape cemetery, yet transforms those practices with contemporary media—music and film. Places in which this kind of communal life can occur are increasingly difficult to find. In a culture where automobiles are the dominant mode of transportation, especially in a city like Los Angeles with a staggeringly immense network of highways, random interactions in public life of city sidewalks tend not to be significant. In comparison to a compact city, or one in which pedestrian traffic and public transportation bring people into common space with each other, Los Angeles can be a difficult place for shared public life. Earnest interactions are further minimized by the use of smartphones and other portable electronic devices. Within the greater Los Angeles metroplex, there are a handful of exceptional neighborhoods like West Hollywood that have a vibrant pedestrian culture. In most of the city, however, people are transformed into drivers who step out of their vehicles only to move from parking lots to building entrances, and sidewalks cannot serve the important function of creating public life for residents. Community is not merely about the demarcations of physical space, such as a boundary street separating Hollywood from West Hollywood, but must also refer to a social network of support and shared experience. The abstracted communities of shared interest have much in common with geographic communities of shared space.

Hollywood Forever, when used for leisure activities, can temporarily serve as a locale for much-needed communal experiences outside of the spaces of home and work. Social discomfort with the cemetery, however, can be a barrier for Cinespia to create an opportunity for Hollywood Forever to serve as a third place. While there are those who object to the idea of watching a film in the cemetery and refuse to participate in Cinespia, others get past their trepidation with encouragement from friends who have already attended. Community is also reinforced by a gathering of a fan community, which often occurs coincidentally at Cinespia. The appreciation for a particular film, and the desire to watch it with a crowd of enthusiastic viewers, can draw individuals to Cinespia. Anticipating a favorite film can alleviate some of the dissonance moviegoers might experience with regard to watching a film in a place normally associated with grief and sorrow. Emotional contagion—from the relaxed tenor of the crowd and the pleasures of moviegoing—helps to transform the cemetery into simply another place to watch a movie. The cemetery is then experienced as a pleasurable space, and if one returns to it for a funeral or to commemorate the death of a loved one, the positive memories of Cinespia may make mourning less difficult. Some visitors find themselves surprised by how comfortable they become spending time at the cemetery.

Cinespia is not unique in offering outdoor entertainment or classic movies; in fact, Angelenos are well-practiced in enjoying both. What makes the film series distinctive is its location at Hollywood Forever. Cemeteries have played host to performances of live music and plays, but Cinespia is the first film series to find its home in a cemetery. Every Saturday night throughout the summer, Hollywood Forever is a different space; there are ways that the film defines the space in which it is shown. The screening of teen comedy *Fast Times at Ridgemont High* created a different atmosphere than the dark drama *Silence of the Lambs* did the following Saturday. Because Cinespia screens classic films and cult classics, watching a film at the cemetery can be an experience of the simultaneity of the past and the present. Hollywood Forever, then, is a space of multiple temporalities. Yet for those who attend Cinespia, there are material ways in which the experience of the cemetery is always the same: the feel of the grass, the familiar layout of the mausoleums and tombstones, or the Hollywood sign in the hills in the distance. The memories of films seen earlier in the summer or during a previous summer do work toward creating a sense of place for the visitor returning to Hollywood Forever.

Cinespia, Nostalgia, and the Drive-in

Cinespia is a nostalgic endeavor, recalling both cemetery traditions and drive-in movies, although it is unlikely that the cinephiles and casual moviegoers who visit Hollywood Forever on Saturdays in the summer are familiar with the leisure uses of cemeteries for generations past. Rural cemeteries were treasured for the way many of them functioned as city parks, providing both open greenspace and public exhibits of art. Regarding Mt. Auburn, the first rural cemetery, Sloane (1991) notes: "Families eagerly purchased lots for $60, expecting to enjoy the beauty of the lot long before the need to bury a relative and for generations to come" (p. 53). Picnicking in the cemetery was a frequent pleasure when few other public spaces were available, during a time when death was not so far removed from everyday life. When people died at home and the family prepared the body for burial, laying out on the grass in the cemetery on a summer day did not carry the discomfort that many experience today. Despite the general cultural discomfort with cemeteries, Hollywood Forever's vast and welcoming lake and the Garden of Legends surrounding it create a peaceful environment for mourners and tourists alike. The area is gently cordoned off after hours for Cinespia, yet adds to a warm atmosphere, made festive with film-appropriate decorations. The reflecting pool in front of the Fairbanks sarcophagus is a focal point of display for Cinespia, with balloons, floating candles, or for the 2016 Slumber Party, an oversized beach ball and a dozen colorful beach umbrellas to create a "weekend away" ambiance. This area sees significant pedestrian traffic on movie nights because the Cinespia photo booth is adjacent to the Fairbanks memorial. The photo booth is also themed to match the film being screened, such as a carnival backdrop complete with a merry-go-round and red convertible to recall the final scene of *Grease* when the 1978 fan favorite was screened at Hollywood Forever.

Moviegoing-as-event is further reinforced with music. The cemetery gates typically open around dusk, giving hundreds of pairs and small groups of moviegoers time to find their spot on the lawn, set up their blanket and picnic, purchase snacks, or visit the photo booth before the movie begins. There may also be an opportunity to get to know your temporary neighbors on the lawn. In *L.A. Weekly*, Dani Katz (2015) writes about the "cool mom" seated next to her offering a plastic cup of red wine at a screening of *Hard Day's Night*: "Jill introduced herself as soon as her clan plopped down next to me. Matt, her husband, is an avid reader. It's their girls' first time here, and they're really into John Lennon. I've known the family for all of five minutes, and we're already in love." The established atmosphere of Cinespia is a friendly environment of sharing public space, and sometimes snacks and wine, with people sitting nearby. Katz notes that "there's even a cute deejay girl spinning a pitch-perfect assortment of swinging 1960s classics," as DJs have long been a part of Cinespia, recalling drive-in traditions. Guest DJs like actor Elijah Wood or musician Questlove bring an added touch of celebrity to the events.

Celebrity sightings are not uncommon at Cinespia. From David Beckham and Gordon Ramsay to Drew Barrymore or Jessica Biel, many celebrities who make their homes in Los Angeles will join the crowds at the cemetery. Cinespia founder John Wyatt often arranges for directors and actors to introduce their films. Paul Reubens is a much-beloved Cinespia guest star, as he has visited the cemetery during different seasons to welcome visitors to the screening of *Pee-wee's Big Adventure*. Reubens developed the character Pee-wee Herman—a quirky, childlike man who always wears the same suit and bowtie—while he was a member of the improvisational comedy troupe The Groundlings in Los Angeles. Following the success of the film, Reubens developed the Saturday morning children's program *Pee-wee's Playhouse*. The series aired on CBS from 1986 to 1991 and attracted a large college-age audience in addition to children. When *Pee-wee's Big Adventure* was screened at Cinespia in 2005, Reubens phoned in an introduction, which John Wyatt broadcast over the public address system. In 2006, *Pee-wee's Big Adventure* sold out—an unusual event at Cinespia at the time, although in subsequent years it became typical for every screening to have a full house. Many disappointed fans were turned away at the cemetery gates, but those who arrived in time to be admitted were treated to a cast reunion, as Paul Reubens, E.G. Daily, and other members of the cast were in attendance. After the event, an attendee wrote enthusiastically about the screening:

> Now the gates opened up at 7:30 and there was already a huge crowd, and I mean huge! It was going to be a sell out night. . . . So when we were all together we enjoyed our picnic and right at 9pm they started the show . . . with some introductions at first . . . Paul Reubens, Pee-wee himself was there! Everyone stood up and cheered. He was so cool, was pretty excited to be there. . . . Seeing the movie was so much fun. This was one of the best crowds to watch with too. When Pee-wee was in Texas and sings everyone watching clapped along and sang "Deep in the Heart of Texas." We had our own fun reciting lines amongst ourselves.
>
> ("Pee Wee")

The familiarity with the script and scenes and the shared experience of clapping along with "Deep in the Heart of Texas" reinforce and reflect the feelings of community among fans and moviegoers that makes Cinespia a popular outing, one weekend after the next.

Running alongside the novelty of Cinespia is the resurrection of traditions from the drive-in movie theater. Like the drive-in, the pleasures of Cinespia far exceed merely watching a movie. Visitors are welcome to bring their own food, beer, and wine, and many take great pleasure in a lavish picnic spread. Cinespia also provides a concession stand with popcorn, candy, and drinks, typical of any movie theater. Music, along with the playful interaction of moviegoers lining up for the photo booth and chatting in the time leading up to the film, creates a festive environment reminiscent of the drive-in. From a peak of 4,063 drive-in theaters in 1958, the number of drive-ins fell from 2,507 in 1987 to only 321 nationwide by 2016 (drive-ins.com, 2016). Yet the drive-in remains a part of the cultural imaginary and has been presented to a younger audience through mediated experiences such as *Grease*, *The Outsiders*, and several video games including *SimCity 2000* and *Grand Theft Auto: San Andreas* that feature drive-in scenarios. Nostalgia for the drive-in is rooted in a yearning for an idyllic communal film-going experience, in which each individual or group occupies their own private space within the context of a larger public setting. This experience was not broadly available to, and is subsequently idealized for, most members of Generation X and Millennials, who are largely representative of those who attend Cinespia.

Svetlana Boym's (2001) explanation in *The Future of Nostalgia* provides insight into how the cemetery, not previously a site for moviegoing, can take the place of the drive-in theater:

> At first glance, nostalgia is a longing for a place, but actually it is a yearning for a different time—the time of our childhood, the slower rhythms of our dreams. In a broader sense, nostalgia is a rebellion against the modern idea of time, the time of history and progress. The nostalgic desires to obliterate history and turn it into private or collective mythology, to revisit time like space, refusing to surrender to the irreversibility of time that plagues the human condition.
>
> (p. xv)

To see Cinespia as emulating the drive-in is to understand the desire to "revisit time like space," rather than to seek out a particular space in which a feeling of the past is situated. As teenagers and twentysomethings, GenXers saw the transformation of broadcast television to cable, the format shift from audio cassette to CD, and the decline of the drive-in accompanied by the proliferation of multiplex theaters, often attached to shopping malls. With its small seats and cramped screening rooms, the multiplex is convenient and suburban, and only remotely recalls the rich history of moviegoing-as-event, whether at the picture palace or the drive-in.

While much has been written about nostalgia as a wasteful attachment to the past, Michael Dwyer (2015) argues for a positive view. He writes that "nostalgia must be understood not as a reduction or denial of history but as a fundamentally *productive* affective engagement that produces new historical meanings for the past as a way of reckoning with the historical present" (p. 22, italics original). Cinespia can be understood as creating layers of affect, for the cemetery, the moviegoing experience, and the films that are screened. The collective pleasure of moviegoing is prevalent throughout the greater Los Angeles area, as several outdoor film series have seen success through emulating Cinespia and its antecedents.

Drop-in drive-ins dot the landscape of Los Angeles, inspired by the Santa Cruz Guerilla Drive-In collective. More of a walk-in or bike-in than a drive-in, the Santa Cruz initiative used mobile technologies to create a temporary screening space. Originally organized via e-mail, members of the collective gathered in designated spaces to project films for free. This reclamation of public space was intended to subvert the consumer culture in which the city is saturated. According to its Facebook page, the Guerilla Drive-in was an "outdoor movie theater under the stars that springs up unexpectedly in the fields and industrial wastelands. Beyond showing great free movies year-round and bringing a broad community together, part of our mission is reclaiming public space and transforming our urban environment."

The gatherings in Santa Cruz inspired MobMov, or mobile movie, "the drive in that drives in." The concept of MobMov is similar to that of a traditional drive-in, but the film is projected from a parked vehicle and audio is carried on an FM radio frequency. Potential participants are informed through social media when a screening is scheduled and where it will occur. The locations are deliberately random, and the ephemerality of the event is in part what makes it appealing. Pop-up movies like MobMov, with their additional appeal of feeling clandestine, are increasingly popular in Los Angeles. Series like the Echo Park Film Center's Filmmobile bring lesser-known films to public spaces where the selected setting has meaning connected to the film. For example, a free screening of *Murs Murs*, Agnes Varda's documentary about street art in Los Angeles, took place in the parking lot of Dino's Burgers in the primarily Mexican-American Boyle Heights neighborhood. Like Cinespia, a trace of the event remains in the memory of those who attend; the space is marked as one in which a clandestine pleasure took place although no physical evidence remains.

Several outdoor cinema series that more closely emulate the drive-in have developed in Los Angeles since Cinespia began in 2002. In the summer of 2007, Angel City Drive-In began screening films in the parking lot of the Alexandria Hotel in downtown Los Angeles. Built in 1906, the hotel provided residence for many film stars in the early years of the industry and was the site chosen by Douglas Fairbanks, Mary Pickford, D.W. Griffith, and Charlie Chaplin to announce the formation of United Artists in 1919. The Angel City Drive-In complemented its screenings with car hop service by members of the roller derby team Angel City Derby Girls as well as Hot Dog on a Stick, the popular snack sold on Venice Beach since 1946. These features, and the location, situated the series as a uniquely Los Angeles experience, yet different from the Hollywood experience of Cinespia. When renovation of the Alexandria Hotel forced the film series to move, it was transformed into Electric Dusk Drive-In, which found its home at the City Market of Los Angeles. Urban development once again led to shutting down EDDI, although the drive-in reopened on a downtown community college campus in 2016.

In addition to Cinespia, the two largest outdoor film series in Los Angeles are Street Food Cinema and Eat|See|Hear, both of which use portable screens at various venues to transform existing public spaces into temporary outdoor moviegoing sites. Performance studies scholar Diana Taylor (2003) brings together ideas of cultural memory and performativity to point to memory as embodied. She argues that "it is impossible to think about cultural memory and identity as disembodied. The bodies participating in the transmission of knowledge and memory are themselves a product of certain taxonomic, disciplinary, and mnemonic systems" (p. 86). Following Taylor, the ritual practices of moviegoing can be understood as embodied memories, whether waiting in line to purchase tickets, getting popcorn, or experiencing the moment when the lights dim to indicate the beginning of the film. At outdoor screenings, moviegoers have similar repeated, embodied experiences, from locating a spot and spreading a blanket to finding one's way back to the parking lot after the screening. These practices become known and familiar because people engage them as they participate in moviegoing. As a ritual practice, both the routines and the deviations from them are comforting, and enable those who attend outdoor movies to create a meaningful sense of place. Screening an oft-watched beloved film of any genre enhances the possibility of creating an embodied ritual, and the knowledge that audience members carry away with them.

With the growing popularity of streaming services, cable and satellite television, and the burgeoning market for home theater technology, watching movies at home can be a convenient and high-quality alternative to the multiplex. What is missing, of course, is the company of others and the pleasure of cinema as a shared experience. Surely a comedy seems funnier when others laugh along with us, and home viewing denies the pleasure of enjoying a film with a group of people in a communal setting. The social experience of Cinespia, constituted in part by chance encounters with strangers, is one you cannot get in your living room, regardless of how many friends you have over to watch.

What We Watch

When Cinespia began at Hollywood Forever, John Wyatt intended to provide an opportunity for film buffs to view more obscure, seldom screened Hollywood classics. Cinespia's mission statement, posted on its website shortly after it went live in 2003, states that the film society was "created to bring together the community of film enthusiasts in Los Angeles. We are convinced that Angelenos are still enthusiastic about cinema's great films, including those outside the normal repertory. We are dedicated to showing unusual films in unusual places." Hollywood Forever is an unusual place for screening a film, yet over the years Cinespia's fare has become increasingly mainstream. Along with many of the other outdoor series in Los Angeles, Cinespia features what will be termed "cult contemporary"—films that have achieved a cult following primarily through their accessibility, repeat viewings, and their role as background for audiences watching on home televisions, in elaborate home theaters, and on mobile devices. Cable television, VHS, and later DVD and Blu-ray players made possible constant, immediate access to films.

For earlier generations, going to the cinema provided the only opportunity to see most films, with the exception of those earning enough popular and critical acclaim to be aired on broadcast television. The films themselves remained precious because of limited access to them. Home viewing changed viewers' relationships with film. The made world of a movie became a place that could be visited at one's convenience, and favorite characters were available to populate one's personal screening space on any given day. Movies became more familiar and taken for granted. For audiences who grew up with a steady stream of film, being able to recite every line of dialog from a favorite movie is not uncommon. Why, then, would audiences go to a screening of a movie they know so well?

Even among cult contemporary films, not all texts are familiar to all viewers. Some Cinespia attendees bring their children to screenings of films like *The Muppet Movie* or *Labyrinth*, and many bring friends to see movies from decades-worth of award-winning cinema that may not be familiar to everyone. The pleasure of sharing a favorite film with a friend or partner can create a strong sense of shared values and meanings. Classic film noir, from *Double Indemnity* (1944) to *Detour* (1945), is standard Cinespia fare, and every season also has included a film directed by Alfred Hitchcock. The frequency of Hitchcock screenings led many to the mistaken belief that the renowned director is buried at Hollywood Forever, such as a blogger in Los Angeles who writes, “the main lawn is tombstone-free, but with a turn of my head, I spotted Hitchcock’s grave in the area behind us” (“Star-struck”). There is a large, standing grave marker prominently adorned with the name “Hitchcock” close to the Cinespia viewing area, but it does not mark the director’s film resting place. Alfred Hitchcock was cremated and his ashes were scattered at sea. Director John Huston is, however, interred in the cemetery, and Cinespia occasionally pays tribute to him with screenings of *The Maltese Falcon* or *The Treasure of the Sierra Madre*. Despite the number of actors and directors buried at Hollywood Forever who played important roles in cinema history, few are featured in the Cinespia schedule.

Yet Wyatt still feels strongly about Cinespia’s ability to educate audiences about film history. He says that many younger moviegoers “don’t know these classic films. I’ve had people [at Cinespia screenings] tell me they’ve never watched a black-and-white film before” (Epstein, 2005). About a 2015 screening of Frank Capra’s *It Happened One Night*, he said, “A lot of our audience are millennials. . . . It’s really exciting for us for these kids to discover this. We hope it inspires people, not only to see more of these films, but to do better at what they do. And for all the people out there making films, we’re hoping that this will encourage them to make films that are really great” (Stone, 2016). Because Los Angeles remains a global center for the film industry, the community’s relationship to movies is unique. Classic, contemporary, foreign language, and documentary films are screened daily at dozens of theaters and other locations including universities, libraries, and museums. Cinemagoing thrives in the city because of the cultural capital and financial capital associated with movies.

Cinespia is, like the drive-in before it, more than just a movie. Having been repackaged as an event rather than a film screening, Cinespia appeals to a younger audience as intent on re-experiencing the films they love as on being exposed to the history of Hollywood cinema. The performative nature of Cinespia is one of the pleasures of attending the screening of a familiar favorite. The coded movie lines that are quoted among fans are welcome shout-outs during screenings and are often used in social media posts to point to familiarity with a film. From clapping along with “Deep in the Heart of Texas” during *Pee-wee’s Big Adventure* to clicking together beer bottles along with Luther in the climax of *The Warriors*, audiences enjoy crowd interaction as part of the Cinespia experience. Perhaps the exemplar for audience interaction is midnight movie mainstay *Rocky Horror Picture Show*, where fans perform the film in its entirety while the audience joins in with various activities and shout-outs. Cinespia hosted a fortieth anniversary screening event for *Rocky Horror* on Halloween night in 2015. The props required for audience participation, including rice (tossed at the newlyweds Brad and Janet) and squirt guns (to emulate rain) were permitted at the screening, and costumes were required for admission.

As it does not quite fit the horror genre, *Rocky Horror* broke a Cinespia tradition of screening a horror film like *Carrie*, *Halloween*, or *The Shining* at the end of the season or as a Halloween screening. While discomfort being in the cemetery at night may still be a prevalent cultural attitude, many Cinespia fans find the horror genre particularly thrilling and prefer it to the "tamer" fare offered on the schedule. Horror film fans enjoy the opportunity to confront the unknown and the supernatural and to engage in the suspense of plot and scene for which the genre is known. While there is relief from terror at the end of the film, part of the appeal for horror fans is the lingering images and fear that are difficult to forget. Walking past standing tombstones and mausoleums on the way back to one's car after screening a horror film at Cinespia can intensify the willing viewer's suspension of disbelief.

During its third season of screenings, Cinespia was honored as one of the best entertainment experiences in Los Angeles. A brief description of the film series ends by noting, "There are limits, however. When Wyatt proposed a salute to horror director George A. Romero with a screening of *Dawn of the Dead*, Cassity ruled that zombie films in a cemetery pushed the boundaries of good taste just a little too far" ("Alfresco"). Three years later, however, *Dawn of the Dead* closed the 2006 season. The preview of the film posted on the Cinespia website and distributed via e-mail positions the film as more of an intellectual endeavor than a frightening excursion into the world of the undead: "A blend of humor, thoughtful social commentary and nail-biting suspense, Romero's masterpiece far surpasses the ordinary boundaries of the genre. . . . Hailed by theorists for its social insight and beloved by horror fans, *Dawn* is truly a unique vision which resonates to this day." Romero's first film in the series, *Night of the Living Dead*, opens in a cemetery in which the dead begin to come back to life, ultimately to search for living humans who will be their cannibalistic prey. Originally released in 1968, *Night of the Living Dead* was added to the National Film Registry in 1999. Each year, the National Film Preservation Board selects 25 films for the Registry that are deemed to be "culturally, historically or aesthetically" significant and thus worthy of preservation for future generations (Film Registry). Since then, three other horror films have been added to the Registry: *Halloween* in 2006, *The Exorcist* in 2010, and *Rosemary's Baby* in 2014. All three have been screened at Cinespia. During the 2017 Halloween season, Cinespia commemorated Romero's career with the premier of a newly-restored version of *Night of the Living Dead*. The director oversaw the restoration shortly before his death. While being an innovative cultural practice, this screening marks one of the first instances of an innovative film appearing on the Cinespia roster.

Despite the recognized significance of Romero's work, some Cinespia fans at the time agreed with Cassity's assertion that horror films are not appropriate for Hollywood Forever. "I thought that the organization was created to give us a chance to see some films that wouldn't normally get seen publicly, on a 'big screen.' I'm disappointed that they've decided to go the route of *The Exorcist* and *Dawn of the Dead*," says one moviegoer. "I know it's a fine line, but I believe those films cross it. The audience doesn't seem to have an appreciation for the historical nature of this venue."[2] This argument attests to the manner in which visitors uniquely make meaning of heritage tourism sites. In the early years of Cinespia, many who regularly visited the cemetery enjoyed the opportunity to share its rich history and beauty with others through the summer movie screenings. As the movies began to be emphasized over the significance of the site, cemetery hobbyists felt that the opportunity to engage with an important site were broadly overlooked for a trendy weekend outing.

Although some of the early fans no longer attend screenings at Cinespia, the film series is a summer mainstay in Los Angeles. The success of Cinespia has inspired outdoor movies in parks, public spaces, and open air auditoriums around the country. These events typically feature cult contemporary films, while many outdoor screenings feature films for children to encourage a family outing in community spaces. A handful of cemeteries have had occasional film screenings that have often been received with some degree of controversy. That Cinespia screenings routinely sell out each weekend is testimony to Hollywood Forever's capacity to enable visitors to feel comfortable spending the evening stretched out on a blanket in the midst of a cemetery.

Notes

1 Unless otherwise noted, all quotes in this chapter are drawn from interviews conducted at Hollywood Forever Cemetery in August 2006, October 2006, and July 2007.
2 This comment is derived from a survey I created and posted on *SurveyMonkey.com*.

References

"Alfresco theater." (2003). *Best of Los Angeles*. Retrieved from https://web.archive.org/web/20130123204131/http://cinespia.org/_press/bestofla.pdf

Boym, S. (2001). *The future of nostalgia*. New York, NY: Basic Books.

Dwyer, M. D. (2015). *Back to the fifties: Nostalgia, Hollywood film, and popular music of the seventies and eighties*. New York, NY: Oxford University Press.

Epstein, R. (2005, May 26). Tinsel and tombstones. *Los Angeles City Beat*. Retrieved from https://web.archive.org/web/20090123133321/www.lacitybeat.com/cms/story/detail/?id=2154&IssueNum=103Jackson

Jackson, J. B. (1980). *The necessity for ruins and other topics*. Amherst: University of Massachusetts Press.

Katz, D. (2015, July 15) Hollywood Forever cemetery movies sell out every weekend because douches don't go. *L.A. Weekly*. Retrieved from www.laweekly.com/arts/hollywood-forever-cemetery-movies-sell-out-every-weekend-because-douches-dont-go-video-5800562

Oldenburg, R. (1999). *The great good place: Cafés, coffee shops, bookstores, bars, hair salons and other hangouts at the heart of a community*. New York, NY: Marlow & Co.

Sloane, D. C. (1991). *The last great necessity: Cemeteries in American history*. Baltimore, MD: Johns Hopkins University Press.

Stone, N. (2016, May 13). Cinespia founder on the "magic" of L.A. cemetery screenings, Justin Timberlake, Emma Stone and more (Q&A). *Hollywood Reporter*. Retrieved from www.hollywoodreporter.com/features/cinespia-15th-anniversary-john-wyatt-893397

Taylor, D. (2003). *The Archive and the repertoire: Performing cultural memory in the Americas*. Durham, NC: Duke University Press.

Terhune, T. R. (2004). *Valentino Forever: The history of the Valentino memorial services*. Bloomington, IN: AuthorHouse.

5 Skeletons, Marigolds, and Sugar Skulls

In an interview in the HBO documentary *The Young and the Dead* (2000), Tyler Cassity says cemeterians typically don't welcome Halloween parties—the possibility of inappropriate or offensive behavior by celebrants is considered too significant a risk. Yet because of relationships Hollywood Forever developed with the local business community, Cassity relented, and in 1999 the cemetery hosted a Halloween fundraiser for the Hollywood Chamber of Commerce. "After the past year, and being out here, and the way they presented it to me, I just thought, 'Well, people want to come here on Halloween. There must be a reason,'" Cassity says. As celebrants in hundreds of communities create mock graveyards on their front lawns and trick-or-treaters dress as ghouls and zombies, the cemetery seems the ideal place for a Halloween event. The Chamber's All Hallow's Eve evolved into a popular fundraiser, replete with cemetery tours, food, and music. Yet the public occasion for which Hollywood Forever attracts a tremendous audience is not Halloween but the traditional Mexican holiday Día de los Muertos, or Day of the Dead. Like Hollywood Forever, Día de los Muertos celebrates the dead, inviting them back to spend time among the living on this day when, as it is said, the veil between the worlds of the living and the dead is thinnest.

With an opening procession, exquisite altars, and live music throughout the day, the cemetery's celebration expanded from around 300 people in 1999 to an average of more than 30,000 visitors throughout the day in subsequent years. This makes Hollywood Forever host to the nation's largest event of its kind. The cemetery is transformed into a brightly colored celebratory space rife with altars, booths, dancers, and visitors in full Día de los Muertos attire. Despite the close proximity of Los Angeles to Mexico, as well as the city's large Mexican population, Hollywood Forever's Día de los Muertos celebration could be seen as an instance of cultural appropriation. As a commemorative practice, Día de los Muertos appears to reflect the perspective embraced by Hollywood Forever. In this regard, the act of appropriation can be understood as a positive extension of a specific cultural practice to serve a broader population.

In her book *Day of the Dead in the USA: The Migration and Transformation of a Cultural Phenomenon*, Regina Marchi (2009) argues that Día de los Muertos, as it is celebrated in the United States, is an "invented tradition." While noting that the phrase is often used pejoratively, Marchi says that Día de los Muertos offers "a historically marginalized population cultural resources with which to counter generations of disparagement from the larger society" (pp. 43–44). For Latinos generally and Mexican-Americans specifically, the holiday creates a visually alluring, festive, and spirited celebration that enables a positive cultural depiction and representation.

While serving to bring people together and to encourage a shifting attitude toward the dead, Hollywood Forever's celebration is also an extension of its role as a tourist destination. Día de los Muertos motivated the promotion of tourism in several Mexican communities where visitors come each year to see the parades and altars and to shop for the unique crafts that incorporate brightly colored skulls and skeletons. Kay Turner and Pat Jasper (1993), founders of Texas Folklife Resources who have written extensively about Chicana culture and Día de los Muertos, see the spread of the holiday in the United States rooted in celebrations that evolved into tourist events in Mexican cities and towns. "People from all over the world now stream into . . . Mexico to observe the celebration. Simultaneous with this phenomenon was the rise of interest in the Day of the Dead on this side of the border," Turner and Jasper note. "The trend continued to grow—in fact, it exploded" leading to Day of the Dead exhibits across the U.S. by the late 1980s (p. 133). Although Turner and Jasper do not mention events on the west coast in their study, Self Help Graphics & Art began the first community-wide celebration of Día de los Muertos in Los Angeles in 1972. The procession and community altar organized by Self Help Graphics remains a popular public celebration of the holiday, and many Día de los Muertos events now take place throughout the city.

The roots of Día de los Muertos extend back to the Aztecs and other indigenous pre-Hispanic cultures. The traditional holiday was so deeply ingrained in Aztec culture that it withstood the invasion and cultural imposition of the Spaniards, and continues to be celebrated today. With the forced conversion to Catholicism, the once month-long celebration of Días de los Muertos became associated with All Saints' Day and All Souls' Day, which fall on November 1 and 2 respectively. Although dates vary among different locales, in many Mexican communities, celebrations on November 1 honor children who have died while those who died in adulthood are honored on November 2. Día de los Muertos often functions more like a family reunion than a day of mourning. Families build altars at home and decorate graves at the cemetery, paying tribute and extending a welcome to their dearly departed. The thousands who visit Hollywood Forever do not have the existing personal relationships one finds in a community cemetery where residents and others who have moved away come together on Día de los Muertos to clean the graves of their loved ones, yet a feeling of warmth and personal connection develops as those who have built altars reminisce about their loved ones and share stories with strangers.

Like traditional Mexican and Mexican-American altars, those constructed at Hollywood Forever include candles, marigolds, incense (*copal*), skulls (*Calaveras*), and skeletons (*Calacas*). The sweet scent of marigolds and copal is said to attract the attention of the dead; the combined odor is also said to be similar to the odor of human bones (*La Ofrenda*). Photographs of the dead are typically included, as well as food offerings of *pan de muertos* (bread of the dead), candy, soda, and favorite foods to entice the dead by recalling the pleasures of living. The bright colors of flowers, blankets, garlands, *papel picados* (folded tissue paper cut into designs), and other decorative elements render the altars as welcoming and celebratory rather than mournful. The spirit of Día de los Muertos often tends to be whimsical and humorous, as there is no morbidity or fear of death in Mexican cultures that believe death is a part of life. This is not to say that there is no sense of mourning; rather that mourning can be bittersweet. The Spanish word *ofrenda* is often used to refer to Día de los Muertos altar offerings because of its rich connotation. An artist in Mexico City, interviewed for the documentary *La Ofrenda: The Days of the Dead* (1989) says, "The word *ofrenda* has a very special meaning in our Indian culture and in all cultures. The word *ofrenda* means love, and love has no price." Love is an inherent aspect of building the altar and preparing for Día de los Muertos because it is time spent thinking about, talking about, and creating something for a loved one. Building an altar takes time, which becomes time-out-of-time in which one is engaged in the past, steeped in memory. This immersion is similar to Mihaly Csikszentmihalyi's (2008) concept of flow, a state of optimal experience in which "concentration is so intense that there is no attention left over to think about anything irrelevant, or to worry about problems. Self-consciousness disappears, and the sense of time is distorted" (p. 71). When the continuity of clock-time is temporarily suspended, the stories of the past saturate the present. For those who decide to build altars at Hollywood Forever, Día de los Muertos creates an opportunity to make space in daily life to stop and commemorate their loved ones. This opportunity is significant in a culture that largely feels more comfortable leaving the dead in the past.

Día de los Muertos celebrations in Los Angeles are among the largest in the nation, as nearly half the city's population self-identifies as Hispanic or

Latino. Los Angeles has a long history of celebrating the holiday. Self Help Graphics & Art, a nationally-recognized gallery and art center in East Los Angeles, held its first Día de los Muertos celebration in 1972 and has influenced the evolution of the city's observance of the holiday ever since. More than 3,000 Angelenos participate in Self Help's procession and blessing of the altars, and contribute to a community altar. Workshops and classes are offered leading up to Día de los Muertos, focused on educating children and the rest of the community through creating *calavera* masks, paper flowers, and other crafts used in the celebration. Through this creative, embodied experience, those who attend workshops become participants in Self Help Graphics' commemoration, tying themselves into the procession and the altar and becoming part of this community of celebrants. Events throughout the city feature live music, performances of traditional dance, altars, processions, artwork, and food. Exhibitions and workshops are held at art galleries, community centers, restaurants, and in neighborhoods in the greater Los Angeles area. Hollywood Forever's celebration, then, is one of many, similar to the way many groups within a community organize their own Fourth of July festivities. But it is the only cemetery in the city that organizes an official Día de los Muertos event. The appeal of inviting the dead to visit with their living relatives reflects Hollywood Forever's philosophy that the focus of the cemetery and the funeral should be on what is colloquially referred to as the "dash between the dates" of birth and death. As a holiday that remembers the dead and sees continuity in life lived, Día de los Muertos is fittingly celebrated at Hollywood Forever.

The cemetery's celebration is organized primarily from within the Latino community. Members of the large Oaxacan community who live in the neighborhood surrounding Hollywood Forever participate as altarists and performers (Quinones, 2006, para. 15). Yet many of those who build altars and attend Día de los Muertos are non-Latinos who are adopting and adapting the practices of another culture for their own purposes. If those outside of the Latino community embrace the idea that the dead still have an active presence in the everyday lives of the living, does their act of cultural appropriation do harm to the traditions of Día de los Muertos? In a multiethnic city like Los Angeles, where people from diverse cultures and nations are learning to live together, can celebrating Día de los Muertos create a common ground in which understanding across cultures can flourish?

As Día de los Muertos blends respect and humor, the celebration at the cemetery blends Mexican tradition with Hollywood kitsch. The hundreds of altars over the years honor and remember the personal, the political, and the famous. Latinos and non-Latinos build altars to invite the return of their loved ones. Typical of the political altars is one dedicated "To our sisters who were murdered in Ciudad Juarez." In 2016, an expansive, lush altar dedicated to the victims of the Pulse nightclub shooting was displayed at the entryway to the cemetery. Other altars are adorned with photographs of Rudolph Valentino, Che Guevara, Frida Kahlo, Elvis Presley, or Jimi Hendrix. One could argue, as Thomas Lynch does, that recalling the lives of the stars we admire is a convenient stand-in for truly mourning our loved ones. Lynch (2000) notes that the intense media focus on celebrity deaths allows us to grieve for distant strangers in ways far more manageable that contending with the death of a relative or close friend:

> With round-the-clock coverage on three cable channels and network news magazines and special reports, no one need change their schedules, put on a suit, order flowers, bake a casserole, go to the funeral home or church. . . . The catharsis is user-friendly, the "healing" home delivered. "Being there" for perfect strangers has never been easier.
>
> (p. 194)

Lynch implies that experiencing the public death of a celebrity is not truly grief and serves little purpose beyond "morbid curiosity." Rather than filling in for personal grief, mourning the death of a celebrity could prepare us to learn the scripts of death and dying. Could the time spent reflecting at the celebrity gravesite be a way to open opportunities for personal grief? The blending of altars honoring loved ones and celebrities at Hollywood Forever indicates the possibilities.

Inspiring the Creatives

The night before the 2006 Día de los Muertos celebration, Arturo Vega was at Hollywood Forever, busily building an altar to honor the members of the Ramones who have died. The altar was on the small expanse of grass next to the cenotaph memorializing Johnny Ramone; along with Johnny and Dee Dee Ramone, Vega honored Joey Ramone, who died in 2001 and is buried in Lyndhurst, New Jersey. Vega was accompanied by Fayette Hauser, a founding member of the cross-dressing performance troupe the Cockettes, who is now a costume designer and photographer. Vega and Hauser both knew the Ramones in the band's earlier years: Hauser performed comedy routines at CBGB, where the Ramones first played, and Vega's apartment in New York City was a gathering place for the band and their friends. Shortly after the Ramones began playing together, Dee Dee and Joey Ramone both found themselves homeless and would often stay at Vega's loft. In his memoir *Lobotomy: Surviving the Ramones*, Dee Dee Ramone (2000) described Vega as "some kind of a mad, but very talented, artist. And very cool too. He saw punk as some sort of a brand new canvas to splash paint on. He became the Ramones lighting director, T-shirt designer, and graphic artist and toured with the band for a long time" (pp. 97–98). As a close friend and artistic director for the band, Vega carried on the Ramones' legacy through his *Ramonesworld* website, through events at Hollywood Forever, and as an often-interviewed expert on the band, until his death in 2013.

Altars typically include the foods and drinks enjoyed by those being remembered, and the chocolate soft drink Yoo-hoo, a Ramones favorite, was featured prominently as an offering at the first Ramones altar in 2005. Like other traditional altars, the Ramones were honored with candles, marigolds, skulls, and *copal*. On his website, Vega (2005) wrote that he was "very excited to be able to do something that united Johnny, Joey and Dee Dee in front of thousands of old and new fans. I didn't know what to expect and the scope of the festival took me by surprise, . . . more than 10,000 spectators, dozens of performers singing and dancing and an atmosphere of wild carnival all over the place." Visitors thronged the market stalls to purchase authentic Día de los Muertos souvenirs and Mexican artworks, and many Ramones fans left room in their shopping bags for t-shirts bearing the iconic Ramones logo that Vega designed.

Throughout the day and into the night, fans paid their respects at the Ramones altar. As the strains of "I Want to Be Sedated" mixed with the sounds from nearby musical and dance performances, the space surrounding the altars for Johnny, Dee Dee, and Joey took on a bittersweet atmosphere. Like Vega, fans were excited by the opportunity to pay homage to the artists they admire yet wistful to reflect not only on their contribution to punk culture but also their untimely deaths. Music, especially in a subculture like punk, is closely linked to identity formation, and fans feel a personal connection to the musicians whose creative work and public personae offered powerful models to emulate.

For Fayette Hauser (personal communication, October 27, 2006), the Ramones altar and Johnny Ramone's cenotaph are a manifestation of Hollywood Forever's willingness to encourage creative methods of commemoration. A long history of unusual monuments precedes Cassity's purchase of and influence over the cemetery—beyond the typical standing monuments are the memorial for Tyrone Power, a white granite bench with a book propped on one end; the elaborate Fairbanks sarcophagus; and the grave marker of Carl Bigsby, which is an exact scale replica of an Atlas rocket. Bigsby, who died in 1959, had no relationship to the space program beyond seeing it as a metaphor for his own successes. Etched on the marker is the following explanation: "The Atlas, pioneer in space, here symbolizes the lifetime activities of Carl Morgan Bigsby, a recognized leader in many phases of the graphic arts. He, too, was a pioneer." The whimsical memorial was one of many that charmed Hauser when she would visit the cemetery with friends in the 1980s. "When I first moved here," she said, "we used to come here all the time because it had all the statuary. We used to take pictures here. . . . We used to play here, like 20 years ago. We liked it because it was old Hollywood. The old film stars are here, and the silent film stars, and there was great statuary."

When Hauser's dear friend Tomata du Plenty (born David Xavier Harrigan) died in 2000, Hollywood Forever immediately came to mind as the appropriate place for his interment. Hauser and du Plenty had a long history together, having both been members of the Cockettes and the Seattle-based performance troupe Ze Whiz Kidz, sharing an apartment, and then moving with other former Cockettes to New York, where they performed at CBGB and other clubs. Du Plenty went on to form the punk rock band the Screamers and is also known for his work as a painter, playwright, and performance artist. The Columbarium was one of du Plenty and Hauser's favorite places at Hollywood Forever, and his ashes are now inurned in a niche there. She said that designing the niche helped her to cope with du Plenty's death:

> It was part of the grieving process for me in that I loved him so deeply and it was tragic and sudden when he died. It took me a month to do it, to figure it out, to get it all together. Because you know they open [the niche] once, and you put it in, and that's it. So I really had to think it through. You can't fuss around with it. There's no fiddling. I did a lot of thinking about it. I found an antique box for him, and he was an artist, so I decoupaged his artwork on it. There's pictures of him on it, because he also had a band that was really popular—he had a lot of different artistic careers.

Du Plenty's niche is similar in spirit to the altars that line the main roadways of the cemetery for Día de los Muertos. Against a backdrop of rich, red, satiny cloth, shot through with strands of gold, are six photographs of du Plenty depicting various incarnations of his creative work. The artwork Hauser chose to decorate the black antique box she found is provocative and colorful, reflecting du Plenty's personality and creative endeavors as a means of commemoration. Opportunities to create evocative cremation niches are not typically welcome at other cemeteries. Hollywood Forever enables both casual visitors and loved ones to remember the idiosyncrasies and passions of those who are commemorated in the cemetery's memorial niches.

Celebrating Celebrity Connections

The celebrity ties to Hollywood Forever carry over to Día de los Muertos as well. A creative approach to ideas of what comprises family inspires some altarists to pay tribute to the celebrities they admire. Celebrity altars are especially fitting for Hollywood Forever, where fans make pilgrimages throughout the year to spend time at the final resting places of actors, musicians, and entertainers significant to them. Sparrow Morgan, founder of the Fairbanks Memorial celebration at Hollywood Forever, chose a "Don Juan" theme for her 2006 Día de los Muertos altar, honoring Douglas Fairbanks, Sr., John Barrymore, and Errol Flynn, each of whom portrayed the adventurous lover in film. Morgan, whose father was a film editor, grew up in the entertainment industry and has an expansive sense of family based in part on cultural influence. She told the *Los Angeles Times*, "In Hollywood, we have a tendency to adopt other people's legacies, because we don't have much of a history of our own. I feel these people are our ancestors, like they are my family" (Quinones, 2006, para. 6). Through mediated encounters, celebrities both living and dead populate our everyday lives, leading many, like Morgan, to feel a familial affinity with them. As those who build altars in memory of their loved ones have the opportunity to share stories of their lives with visitors to the cemetery, so did Sparrow Morgan tell the captivating histories of these actors who played significant roles in the early years of the film industry. Her tribute is also a performance of fandom that stitches her into the afterlife of Fairbanks, Flynn, and Barrymore. For those who are not familiar with the actors or have not heard their stories, Morgan functions almost like a medium, communicating on behalf of the dead.

Like Morgan, West Hollywood residents Sandy and Matt use Día de los Muertos to celebrate the lives of film stars and have built altars at Hollywood Forever for several years. While they usually discard the items used, Matt recalls that when they created an altar for Rudolph Valentino, two young boys asked for photographs of the silent film star at the end of the night. Matt gladly gave them the pictures and was surprised when they returned, asking for more. When the boys returned for a third time, one of them offered Matt two cigars that his father had sent in appreciation. Within Día de los Muertos traditions, this gifting is analogous to the way in which children will bring food from their family altars to their godparents or other family members after the dead have visited and departed. Garciagodoy (1998) explains that "often the godchildren are charged with taking these baskets [of food the dead have left] to their godparents with whom they may eat before returning home, the baskets filled anew with some of the delicacies that were on the godparents' altar" (p. 14). Not only is a tradition evoked, but the children also take home photographs of Valentino as a souvenir. The Latin Lover enters the cultural imaginary and occupies a place in the landscape of memory that includes Día de los Muertos. In a highly mediated culture, learning about the world occurs through both lived experience and mediated encounters, which intermingle at the cemetery where so many media figures are represented and commemorated. For the boys, the Valentino photographs function as a material marker of their experience at the cemetery—one that includes participating in commemoration of their family's loved ones, enjoying the spectacle of dance and music, and, by virtue of exchanging gifts with Matt, Rudolph Valentino himself. Their world is populated by these objects and performances, and they will understand themselves in part through their roles in the day's events.

Those who honor their loved ones are creating altars in defiance of a cultural perception that we should "be done with" our dead; after a prescribed time of mourning is completed, we are expected to leave the dead in the past. Looking at photographs and watching videos of loved ones, or even visiting the grave frequently, is thought of as an indulgence. Engaging to excess with the intimate dead is frowned upon as an indication that one is living in the past and not properly coping with death. While indulging ourselves with memories of our dearly departed is scorned, the constant present absence of dead celebrities is unquestioned. Taylor (2003) uses the death and funeral of Lady Diana Spencer as an example of the lively afterlife of celebrity: "The remains, in this spectacle, take on a life of their own—so much so that one tabloid photo montage has Di looking on at her own funeral from the corner with a bittersweet smile, one more witness to an event that has overtaken her" (p. 142). Taylor argues that "politically and symbolically, we haven't seen the end of her," as Diana's image continues to be socially productive after her death (p. 142). With Prince William and Kate Middleton being newsworthy public figures, the aura of Diana is often brought into the conversation. What might be gained if we allow the stories and images of our loved ones to circulate after death? We can learn a sense of continuity within our families and within the cultures we are part of. Rather than thinking of the past as a series of events, images, and narratives, we can place ourselves in the trajectory from the past into the present by placing our forbears within those narratives.

Celebrating Community

The Día de los Muertos celebration at Hollywood Forever is a performance of cultural memory; altars that commemorate various celebrities, artists, and loved ones keep these individuals, their histories, and their acts in circulation. Traditional Día de los Muertos celebrations similarly keep the ancestors alive for the family, but at Hollywood Forever the notion of community extends beyond family to include the consuming public who visit the cemetery for this event. Histories of Latino culture, both personal and public, are communicated through the display of altars, performances of dance and music, and an art exhibition in the Cathedral Mausoleum. Taylor (2003) would argue that this display is essential to locating the presence and impact of Latino culture in the United States. She reminds us that

> Latino/as became the largest minority in the United States, though no one seemed to notice. They, like [television astrologer] Walter [Mercado], are depicted as completely invisible, unlocatable, and/or utterly performatic. They still drop out of most discussions on race. . . . Who knows who Latino/as are or what they have accomplished in the United States? Which archives house their histories, writings, and artistic achievements?"
>
> (p. 123)

As a public event attended by thousands, Hollywood Forever's Día de los Muertos celebration enables access to those archives that are personal, familial, and often hidden from view. Individuals, objects, and traditions are plucked from the archive and situated, as Taylor posits, in "a repertoire performed through dance, theatre, song, ritual, witnessing, healing practices, memory paths, and the many other forms of repeatable behaviors as something that cannot be housed or contained in the archive" (pp. 36–37). For those who fear their ongoing engagement with personal memories of their loved ones could be seen as indulgent, Día de los Muertos can begin to normalize the idea that the dead remain an active part of the world of the living.

Día de los Muertos altars dedicated to celebrities can also recognize deep personal conviction. An altarist named Jenna built an expansive altar to remember a group of individuals with a specific purpose in mind: to point to the dangers of drug addiction. A multicolored banner announcing "Sex, Drugs, Rock 'n' Roll" streams above a long table covered with a pink cloth. Two dozen small picture boxes, painted in a variety of colors, are arranged on the table. Each box commemorates a public figure from the rock-and-roll scene whose death was linked to drug addiction. A small black box contains a *calaca* representing Sid Vicious, bassist for the Sex Pistols, who died of a heroin overdose in 1979. Atop this box is a pink octagonal box with a skeleton splayed on the floor beside a tiny bathroom sink; this box commemorates Vicious' girlfriend, Nancy Spungen, who died four months before he did. Small framed biographies are arranged next to each box. A box for River Phoenix is on one side of the memorials for Vicious and Spungen; a box for Kurt Cobain is on the other. Jenna notes that "when we're younger, we think that all these rock stars are so cool and drugs are so glamorous. And so this was kind of a fun way of showing what really happens at the end of it." Because of the bright, colorful boxes and frames she uses, appropriate to Día de los Muertos, Jenna feels the anti-drug message may be effective in this context because "it's a bit more playfully done where it's not shoving it down your throat."

The altar was inspired by Jenna's own sobriety and by two friends within the recovery community for whom she made a separate altar nearby. One is Jenna's friend Maureen Nolan, who was sober for seven years and died after a battle with cancer in 2004. The other is the novelist Hubert Selby, Jr., the author of *Last Exit to Brooklyn* and *Requiem for a Dream*, who overcame his addiction to painkillers and heroin some thirty years before his death. "He had been sick for a lot of years," Jenna explains. "He died in his 70s. So people that I knew who knew him for twenty, thirty years—it's always been a thing, like Cubby is dying. But it took really like fifty more years of him living to die. Then my friend got cancer, and he started to watch her come around. And everyone knew she had cancer, but she was living and it really inspired him; that he's got to stop thinking that he's dying. Well, the weird thing is that they both did die [within months of each other], but they kind of both taught each other how to live again." In paying tribute to those who helped her gain sobriety, Jenna hopes to "get people thinking" about the consequences of drug addiction.

The 2007 Día de los Muertos celebration allowed the family of actor Don Adams to get input from fans and visitors on the choice of statuary to mark Adams' grave. The selection of a grave marker would typically be a highly personal decision, as seen in Fayette Hauser's design of Tomata du Plenty's niche in the Columbarium, yet there was dissent among Adams' family members about whether his final resting place should reflect his public or private persona. Adams died in September 2005, yet his grave remained unmarked for more than two years. He played Maxwell Smart, also known as Agent 86, in the Cold War spy comedy *Get Smart* (1965–1970). The series parodied the high tech devices and gadgets of the James Bond movies, such as the telephone embedded in Smart's shoe on which he would awkwardly answer calls. Each episode of *Get Smart* included a variety of gadgets, but the shoe phone is likely the most memorable. A statue of Adams, as Maxwell Smart, taking a call on the shoe phone was one option considered by that family, while others advocated for a more traditional marker of a large angel. The family eventually chose the angel rather than the shoe bust as a grave marker, along with a plaque that features a depiction of Adams with the shoe phone pressed to his ear. Family members know tourists and fans will visit Adams' grave among the many other stops on the celebrity tour of Hollywood Forever. Even among Los Angeles' celebrity-friendly cemeteries, it is difficult to imagine a scenario in which family members would seek public input on commemorating a loved one. This is a testament to the ways Hollywood Forever is used as social space, and conversations about how to memorialize a celebrity can readily occur in a space where visitors are accustomed to talking openly with casual passersby.

Although the Hollywood Chamber of Commerce Halloween fundraiser and the Día de los Muertos celebration are both relatively new to Hollywood Forever, the Art Deco Society of Los Angeles began conducting annual Halloween tours there in 1984. The well-attended tours are conducted by costumed docents stationed at various gravesites who explain the historical and architectural importance of the cemetery and its permanent residents. "Practically all of Hollywood's history can be revisited here," said Frank Cooper, the Art Deco Society board member who initiated the annual tour (Biederman, 1989, para. 1), and the historical appeal takes precedence over the spookiness associated with holding the tour at Halloween. The Art Deco Society is not the only organization to use Halloween as a time to invite visitors to learn more about cemetery history. Prominent cemeteries including Oakland Cemetery in Atlanta, St. Louis #2 in New Orleans, Laurel Hill in Philadelphia, and Brooklyn's Green-Wood Cemetery customize their tours for Halloween presentations, when more visitors typically join the tours. Smaller cemeteries also leverage the Halloween season to bring visitors to tour the grounds. In nearby Long Beach, for example, the Historical Society leads a tour of the city's two oldest cemeteries on Halloween weekend, using costumed volunteers to relate the history of Long Beach through the stories of those interred in the cemetery.

Despite the popularity of Halloween tours, few cemeteries organize official Día de los Muertos events. Hollywood Forever's celebration wins favor from some for precisely the same reasons others find it offensive: the cemetery draws on ancient practices while also incorporating new rituals and expanding the celebration to include a multicultural approach. Critics of Hollywood Forever who see the cemetery appropriating another culture's traditions for its own purposes are not incorrect, but this appropriation can result in a positive reflection of celebrating the dead and inviting the dearly departed to spend time among the living. Hollywood Forever readily benefits by extending itself as a good corporate citizen that invites the Latino community to come together to celebrate a significant holiday. As Día de los Muertos celebrations occur elsewhere in Los Angeles, the cemetery is not offering a unique service but does provide a unique setting which is appropriate to commemorative acts that recall the lives of the dead.

References

Baumel, E. (Producer), Pulcini, R. and Springer Berman, S. (Directors). (2000). *The Young and the Dead.* [Motion picture]. United States: HBO.

Biederman, P. W. (1989, October 27). Cemetery of Stars Not Entirely a Grave Matter Hollywood: Memorial park, subject of Halloween tours, offers a mix of styles to delight the tombstone aficionado. *Los Angeles Times*, 14.

Csikszentmihalyi, M. (2008). *Flow: The psychology of optimal experience*. New York, NY: Harper Perennial.

Garciagodoy, J. (1998). *Digging the days of the dead: A reading of Mexico's Días de Muertos*. Niwot, CO: University Press of Colorado.

Lynch, T. (2000). *Bodies in motion and at rest: On metaphor and mortality*. New York, NY: W. W. Norton & Co.

Marchi, R. M. (2009). *Day of the dead in the USA: The migration and transformation of a cultural phenomenon*. New Brunswick, NJ: Rutgers University Press.

Portilla, L. (Producer and Director) and Munoz, S. (Producer and Director). (1989). *La Ofrenda: The Days of the Dead*. [Motion picture]. United States: LA Direct Cinema.

Quinones, S. (2006, October 28). Making a night of Day of the Dead: The Mexican tradition gets an L.A. twist as even non-Latinos join in at a Hollywood cemetery. *Los Angeles Times*. Retrieved from www.latimes.com/news/local/la-me-dead 28oct28,1,7790642.story.

Ramone, D. D. and Kofman, V. (2000). *Lobotomy: Surviving the Ramones*. Boston, MA: Da Capo Press.

Spindler, A. M. (1998, November 15). Getting In. *New York Times Sunday Magazine*. Retrieved from www.nytimes.com/1998/11/15/magazine/getting-in.html

Taylor, D. (2003). *The Archive and the repertoire: Performing cultural memory in the Americas*. Durham, NC: Duke University Press.

Turner, K. and Jasper, P. (1993). Day of the dead: The Tex-Mex tradition, In J. Santino (Ed.), *Halloween and Other Festivals of Death and Life* (pp. 133–137). Knoxville, TN: University of Tennessee Press.

Vega, A. (2005). Día de los Muertos. Ramoneworld.com. Retrieved from https://web.archive.org/web/20051024035905/www.ramonesworld.com/site/nav.html

6 Conclusion

Expanding the Scope

Any organization—even a cemetery—responds and adapts to changes in the culture at large. For Hollywood Forever, some of those cultural changes have been significant. Having always embraced a perspective that favors celebrating a life lived rather than mourning a loss, Hollywood Forever has played a role in recent transformations in death care, especially with regard to the death positive movement. Advances in technology that have made films always available transformed moviegoing, and Cinespia along with it. In addition, the constant accessibility of information that accompanies mobile technologies has enhanced parasocial relationships with celebrities and other public figures. Once-ridiculed fan communities have become commonplace, and fandom plays a pivotal role in the increasing popularity of Hollywood Forever. Fandom encourages tourism to sites that welcome visitors who are motivated by fan pilgrimages, and this pairs with cultural heritage, a growing sector of the tourism market.

Death Care and the Death Positive Movement

The inevitability of death is a fundamental fact of life. Yet, because of the medicalization of death and the institutionalization of the death care industry, the experience of death has become increasingly foreign and frightening. Coroners, embalmers, and funeral directors take care of the dead, where family members take care of their grief, the requisite paperwork and the settling of accounts. The literal caretaking of the dead was once in the hands of the family, who would clean and dress the body and prepare their loved ones for burial. The transition from "loved one" to "the body" now occurs largely at a distance from family and friends of the deceased.

The notion of "a good death" might strike many as strange, yet is increasingly used in discussions of death and dying as a way to address end-of-life issues in a positive light. If quality of life is an issue that has been in public discourse of decades, quality of death is an extension of that same discussion: what does it take to make death more tolerable and less tragic? It makes sense to think of a good death as part of a life well lived. The convergence of various cultural movements is changing how Americans deal with death. In an increasingly secular society, the rituals of death situated in religious customs are not as frequently employed as they once were. When death enters public discourse, we begin to feel more comfortable talking with our loved ones about funeral arrangements, burial, cremation, and other options. While the idea of a good death is well underway in contemporary culture, there may be less public discussion of quality commemoration. It seems a natural extension—that if we devote ourselves to the best possible experience for both the person dying and the surrounding community of loved ones, should we not also think about how we can facilitate grief? Ultimately, we come to the question: how do you want to be remembered?

Many writing on the death industry (Lynch, 2000; Mitford, 1998; Palmer, 1993) relate incidents in which a family tells a funeral director, "It's what Dad would have wanted," when the funeral arrangements are more likely to reflect what the family wants. In her groundbreaking 1963 book *The American Way of Death*, Jessica Mitford recounts an informal survey conducted by the *San Francisco Chronicle* in which individuals on the street were asked what kind of funeral they wanted. She says the respondents typically wished for inexpensive, simple funerals. In her wry manner, Mitford notes:

> Oddly enough, the funeral men . . . are not particularly worried. After all, these people will not be around to arrange their own funerals. When the bell tolls for them, the practical essentials—selection of a casket and all the rest—will be in the hands of close relatives who will, it is statistically certain, express their sense of loss in an appropriately costly funeral.
>
> (p. 130)

As advances in medicine have allowed many terminally ill individuals to sustain some quality of life, many have worked with their loved ones to decide how they want their funerals to be arranged.

In *The American Way of Death*, Mitford also offered a scathing critique of the funeral industry, from the financial to the psychology manipulations of funeral directors. British-born Mitford was baffled by the insistence on an open casket in American funerals, wondering why family and friends would wish for this final viewing. She blames the "funeral men" for claiming that "mental and emotional solace [can be] achieved for the bereaved family as a result of being able to 'view' the embalmed and restored deceased" (p. 64). Mitford pointedly notes that there is no evidence from psychiatric experts to support these claims. Nonetheless, these ways of dealing with death have become a way of life in the United States. Although the discussions throughout this book show that there is a new consideration of death care practices underway, embalming and burial have been the norm for decades. Many still think of cremation as an innovative practice, even though nearly half the deaths in the United States result in cremation rather than traditional burial. Even more Americans are unfamiliar with natural burial as an option to embalming and burial in a casket and vault. Yet along with the innovative practices at Hollywood Forever, Tyler Cassity is also the co-owner of Fernwood Cemetery, a green cemetery in northern California.

When Cassity purchased Hollywood Memorial Park out of bankruptcy in 1998, he was 27 years old. Cassity's various motivations were connected to one another. As a young gay man living in New York City, Cassity saw the deaths of many contemporaries from AIDS. The deaths of young men, often rejected by their families, brought about new rituals and practices to mark a death. As he and others have noted, those practices often included celebrations instead of somber funerals. Tyler Cassity also tells a story of hearing a cassette tape recording of his grandmother speaking, found shortly after her death. These influences led to the creation of LifeStories, the video biographies that are often shown at funerals at Hollywood Forever. Cassity was in Los Angeles to promote LifeStories to the National Funeral Directors Association when he heard the cemetery was up for auction. In an interview with *New York Times*, he said, "I fell in love with this place immediately. It was a cultural icon full of cultural icons" (Spindler, 1998). Restoring the iconic cemetery included not only repairing the neglected buildings and grounds and reestablishing its reputation, but also returning to the cemetery's primary business of burying and interring the dead.

Hollywood Forever is still an operating cemetery that has expanded its mausoleums and continues to accept new interments. In early 2017, the cemetery received approval to expand an existing mausoleum and build a new structure, creating space for 25,000 crypts and 25,000 cremation niches. The cemetery is a desirable burial site, not only because of the public figures already interred there, but also because of ongoing work to promote it as a significant cultural site. In addition to creating a sense of place and belonging through inviting use of the cemetery as leisure space, Hollywood Forever maintains a liberal policy for creative grave markers and niches. As many lawn park cemeteries traditionally maintain strong restrictions, Hollywood Forever's policies are inviting in a city that prides itself on being one of the world's foremost centers of cultural production. When visitors to the cemetery find the unconventional markers enchanting, they may be drawn to return to the cemetery and to possibly imagine their own gravesites. As sociologist Mark Gottdiener (1996) points out in his study of tourist environments, "individuals or groups use or interpret the constructed space by imputing some meaning or meanings to it. These people may be customers, inhabitants, visitors, or clients, but they are all users of the space in some fashion" (p. 5). Film and television critic Mike Szymanski, who made frequent childhood visits to historic Green-Wood Cemetery in Brooklyn, is now a frequent visitor to Hollywood Forever, often bringing his own young sons with him. Szymanski is both property owner and visitor, as his father's ashes are in a niche in the Abbey of the Psalms mausoleum. Mike and his partner have a plot for themselves across from the Garden of Legends. He says his father has more visitors at Hollywood Forever than he did during the last year of his life, as a visit to the cemetery can function as far more than act of commemoration. Visitors who pay their respects to a loved one also have opportunities to experience both the splendor and the history of the cemetery. Like many who develop a sense of connection to Hollywood Forever, Szymanski appreciates the liberal policies on decorative grave markers and niches. These are, or can be, playful spaces. We may remember our dead fondly, which does not mean we do not remember them reverently as well. Again, remembering lives lived can transform personal and public memory.

The inclusion of cultural icons among those interred at Hollywood Forever continues as well. According to Michael Kammen (2010), the concept of the celebrity cemetery in the United States stretches back to the early rural cemeteries including Mount Auburn in Boston and Brooklyn's Green-Wood.

> When groups of people, cities, privately owned cemeteries, or states contested where the remains of a celebrity should most properly repose, *pride of place* was often at stake. . . . Matters of pride often caused but also resulted from intense rivalries—between regions, states, and families. Then add the commercial competition of newly established cemeteries seeking to become tourist attractions as well as profitable investments. People must buy burial plots, and often they like to be interred where celebrities have already been situated.
>
> (p. 9)

The cemetery at which a celebrity is interred maintains pride of place in perpetuity—while the hometown of some stars are unable to create a public sense of place related to that person, others benefit from the connection. Jayne Mansfield, for example, was born in Bryn Mawr, Pennsylvania, and after her death in 1967, she was interred in the same cemetery as her father in Pen Argyl, about an hour from her birthplace. A devoted fan would need to make a pilgrimage to a rather remote locale to properly pay tribute to Mansfield. With this in mind, the Jayne Mansfield fan club in Los Angeles funded a cenotaph at Hollywood Forever so they and others could make possible the inscription, "We live to love you more each day."

Along with stars from the Golden Age of Hollywood, burials at the cemetery since it was reopened include Estelle Getty, Mickey Rooney, Mel Blanc, and Larry Drake, attracting the interest of a new generation of fans. Yet another recent interment is actor Anton Yelchin, who died in 2016 as the result of an automobile malfunction. Among the 27-year-old actor's roles was his portrayal of Pavel Chekov in the third generation of *Star Trek* films. Considering the intensity of *Star Trek* fandom, it is likely that Yelchin's grave in the Garden of Legends will draw visitors to Hollywood Forever. Interestingly, his gravestone does not have dates of birth and death marked on it, just his name and the word "Forever."

In its continuing effort to focus on celebration rather than mourning, and to make the cemetery a space for leisure and enjoyment, Hollywood Forever is aligned with the growing "good death" movement. From green burial to death cafes that encourage informal conversations about death and dying, the good death movement invites new perspectives. Caitlin Doughty, author of the memoir *Smoke Gets In Your Eyes & Other Lessons from the Crematory*, is a high profile advocate for death acceptance. She organized the Order of the Good Death and opened Undertaking LA, an alternative funeral service that places the dying person and the family at the center of the process of dying. Undertaking LA's office is located on Santa Monica Boulevard, less than a mile away from Hollywood Forever.

Creative Options Through Cremation

When burial is chosen, the body is in a fixed location, chosen either by the person before his or her death or by the surviving loved ones. Before mobility transformed American lifeways and families would stay in one town or city for generations (as is still the case in some instances), the family plot was a typical expectation. People knew they would be buried with their forebears, and everyone in the family knew where they would go to pay their respects. But the stability of home is far less common, complicating burial choices. Blended families complicate burial choices as well—in cases of divorce and remarriage, the notion of a family plot becomes emotionally complex and territorial. Such a choice could cause a permanent schism between family members, resulting in commemoration with bitterness, the antithesis of the expected peaceful outcome. Cremation offers an option—in many instances, cremains are divided among family members so that each can have a means of commemoration. Following her cremation, Dinah Shore's ashes were divided and interred in two different cemeteries. Dividing the ashes can also soothe the dispute of a blended family, for example, enabling a woman who remarries to be buried with both of her husbands.

Some choose to keep cremains as a sacred object while others choose to scatter the ashes in a place imbued with meaning. Traditionally, returning cremains to nature was expected, and ashes were often scattered at sea. Some cemeteries, including Hollywood Forever, have cremation gardens that include options for in-ground burial of cremains or a scattering garden, both of which imply a return to nature. As cremation gains in popularity and becomes commonplace, the options for scattering ashes are increasing, and many are unconventional. For example, a blogger who commemorated her father's death with an altar at the Día de Los Muertos celebration at Hollywood Forever writes that she and her brother "reminisced about our father to thousands of visitors. Once we started, it became easy to talk about him. There were so many quirks that made up his sparkling personality. . . . Invariably, his Ted Williams t-shirt on display sparked the question 'Did he get to see them win?' and guests were disappointed that he hadn't until we pointed out a ticket from Fenway where we illegally spread his ashes."

The desire to scatter ashes has some kinship to cultural moves of letting go of connections to materiality. The choice of mp3 files over CDs and digital pictures over a bookshelf of photo albums makes the compulsion to "keep the bones" seems less demanding, especially as negative cultural perceptions of cemeteries persist. As expected, there is also a significant market for the scattering of ashes beyond the typical burial at sea.

For those who do decide to keep cremation ashes, the formal, traditional urn is now only the beginning of options. Hollywood Forever offers cremation urns for sale, with different charges for cremation depending on whether the container is purchased on site. Columbaria with niches for cremation urns and other memorial artifacts are found in several locations around the cemetery grounds. Artisans and commercial interests have created an extensive market for cremation urns. Everlife Memorials, for example, offers bronze, brass, wood, glass, and ceramic urns, along with cremation jewelry. As Mitford reflected on the postmortem decisions made in the spirit of "it's what Dad would have wanted," one wonders about the conversation that ends with a decision to have ashes divided and kept in a sterling silver pendant in the shape of a football, a music note, or a fishing hook. The implication of cremation jewelry is that the person who chooses this keepsake does so knowing that she or he will be handling the cremains and placing them carefully in the very small opening of the pendant. Not only does it seem like a significant responsibility, it also implies comfort with the ashes. These customs that may be critiqued as bizarre or disrespectful revert back to times before the medicalization of death, when mourning jewelry that featured bits of bone or hair was commonplace.

The cultural traditions of death and mourning fade and are brought back into circulation depending on other cultural attitudes. Alongside a revival in the popularity of mourning jewelry, Hollywood Forever is working to bring back a perception of the cemetery as a cultural space for art, leisure, and public commemoration.

Cemetery as Cultural Center

In a May 2007 interview, Jay Boileau, executive vice president at Hollywood Forever, told the *Los Angeles Times*, "Part of our business plan to save a bankrupt cemetery was to make it a cultural center. To bring people back by hosting a variety of events" (Lee, 2007, para. 22). Hollywood Forever's notion of a cultural center is expansive, including not only historical tours and summer performances of Shakespeare plays but also a variety of popular culture events.

As the Valentino memorial screening inspired John Wyatt, so has Cinespia inspired others to use the Fairbanks Lawn as a screening site. Among the screenings for which Hollywood Forever has been a thematically appropriate venue are the final episode of the HBO series *Six Feet Under* in August 2005, the premiere of ABC's series *Pushing Daisies* in 2007, and the death-filled Season 7 premiere of *The Walking Dead* in late 2016. In the intervening years, another event with a strong connection to Hollywood Forever became an annual tradition.

In 2005, Johnny Ramone's widow Linda and longtime Ramones artistic director Arturo Vega organized a tribute and prostate cancer benefit at Hollywood Forever with a summer screening of the 1979 cult classic *Rock 'n' Roll High School*. The Johnny Ramone Tribute is designed to commemorate the band, including Johnny (born John Cummings) and Dee Dee Ramone (born Douglas Colvin), whose gravesite is at the opposite end of the path from Johnny Ramone's cenotaph. Within this fan community, each Ramones event also provides ample opportunity for celebrity sightings and autographs. Among those who have been in attendance to honor the Ramones and to share their reminiscences are former bandmate Marky Ramone; musicians Henry Rollins and Eddie Vedder; and actors PJ Soles, Clint Howard, and Mary Woronov who appeared in *Rock 'n' Roll High School*.

The screenings are a site for the performance of fandom and participation in punk culture, enhancing the significance of Ramone's memorial for returning visitors. The prominent placement of Johnny Ramone's cenotaph makes the Ramones a cultural institution in perpetuity. The statue is located on the edge of the Garden of Legends, across from the Fairbanks sarcophagus and the Cathedral Mausoleum, and stands out on the landscape for tourists looking for celebrity gravesites at Hollywood Forever. As visitors retell the stories of the Ramones to their friends and children, the cenotaph prompts the circulation of these narratives into the culture beyond the cemetery gates.

Hollywood Forever is a popular venue for concerts, beginning with a performance by Bon Iver on the Fairbanks Lawn in 2009. Jay Boileau told *Los Angeles Magazine* (Deulund, 2014) that the concert was organized as a "sleepover," with movies and music throughout the night and the band taking the stage at sunrise. "A really thick fog rolled in around 4:30 a.m., which we thought was going to be a problem, but it actually made the concert much more beautiful. People still talk about that concert. It's legendary," Boileau said (para. 7). Concerts and other events also bring visitors year round to the Masonic Lodge on the cemetery grounds. Built in 1931 and listed on the National Register of Historic Places, the Masonic Lodge is an intimate and popular performance venue. Passing through the cemetery gates for a concert in the Masonic Lodge normalizes the act of visiting the cemetery. A live performance, in a space strongly associated with the dead, also transforms the aura of Hollywood Forever as the space becomes part of a different kind of memory for those who attend concerts and other events.

Fans continue to return to Hollywood Forever to pay tribute to the artists who inspire them. The gravesite pilgrimage remains popular, particularly with the unexpected deaths of several rock music stars. As public discussions of those deaths continue, journalist Jason Tabrys (2017) offers an explanation for the depth of grief fans experience when celebrities die. Reflecting on the death of Chris Cornell, Tabrys writes, "Whether young or old, vibrant and full of life or wasting away before our eyes, the death of a beloved artist always comes on like a violent squall because, to a degree, those people are frozen in our minds at the point of their greatest impact on us."

Outdoor Movies: Trending in Los Angeles and Beyond

When Cinespia began in 2002, the screenings were initially an expansion of John Wyatt's film club that gradually grew more popular. Within the first few years, tickets to certain films began to sell out. The contemporary cult classic *Pee-wee's Big Adventure*, which included a call-in introduction over the public address system from Paul Reubens, then in-person appearances by Reubens and other actors from the film, became an annual event at Cinespia.

Cinespia creates a temporary but repeating sense of public space at Hollywood Forever. Through the sense of belonging that arises from enjoying the cemetery and staking out "your spot" on the lawn, visitors develop their own personal sense of place and a lasting association with Hollywood Forever. While many viewers leave behind public film screenings for the intimate and private home theater, DVD player, or laptop, Cinespia is a venue that offers an unusual screening experience. The quirky nature of Cinespia, and its location in the cemetery, attracts viewers who may not necessarily be motivated to attend primarily by virtue of the film being screened on any particular night. For others, a Saturday night at the cemetery is driven by the desire to see a favorite film—often a cult classic—at the cemetery or in the company of others who share an appreciation for that film. Some go to Cinespia for the experience itself, as one would go to a particular club or coffeehouse where the ambience, the music, and the clientele create a comfortable sense of belonging. As Cinespia has grown in popularity, some participants who enjoyed the scene, as well as those who enjoyed the intimacy of a smaller gathering in the historic space of the cemetery, have become disenchanted.

Success spawns success, and Angelenos now have a variety of outdoor summer film series from which to choose their weekend evening entertainment. Street Food Cinema and Eat|See|Hear both have screenings at venues across the city, using an immense inflatable screen rather than the fixed space of the mausoleum wall at Hollywood Forever. Although Cinespia screenings are more likely than not to sell out, and the screening area has been expanded to enable larger audiences, some outdoor movie fans feel that the scope of the event should not deter them from attending. Others prefer low key screenings that are less crowded and need not be planned in advance to ensure availability.

Like Cinespia, other outdoor screenings draw on a strong sense of place to create a lasting connection with moviegoers. In other cities, like Austin, Tucson, and Tampa, outdoor movies are screened at culturally and historically significant locations, pairing moviegoing with heritage tourism. These efforts encourage a "tourist in your own town" mentality that invites residents to become familiar with venues in their communities that could in turn bring visitors to spend their time and money locally.

Cultural Heritage

The redevelopment of Hollywood, which coincided with the renovation of Hollywood Forever, depends largely on establishing sites for destination tourism related to the film industry. Among the drive-by tours of stars' homes and the performers dressed as characters looking for photo opportunities in the Chinese Theatre forecourt, the mid-1990s saw the beginning renovation of the Egyptian and El Capitan movie palaces along Hollywood Boulevard. The Hollywood & Highland Center, which includes an homage to D.W. Griffith's 1916 film *Intolerance* by recreating the film's massive archway and elephant sculptures, opened in 2001. Hollywood & Highland is also a tourism destination that invites visitors not only to engage in shopping and leisure activities, but also to recall Hollywood's history and their attachments to it. Some of those attachments are situated in fandom, as Hollywood as an attraction is driven by its ability to function as a material articulation of fandom. As a significant cultural force, fandom draws visitors to Los Angeles and many of its attractions that highlight the film industry as a form of cultural heritage.

Like other celebrity cemeteries, Hollywood Forever serves as a site where heritage intersects fandom. If a cemetery is intended as a site of remembrance, in some circles fandom is precisely that: a place to remember and to perpetuate the lifework of those who are interred there. While Cassity once wished for the likes of Frank Sinatra to choose Hollywood Forever as their final resting place (Spindler, 1998, para. 14) (Sinatra is buried at Desert Memorial Park in Cathedral City), the cemetery has a powerful "B list" appeal that makes it particularly charming for those with nostalgia for old Hollywood. Its status was enhanced in early 2017, when Liza Minnelli had the remains of her mother, Judy Garland, moved from New York to Los Angeles to be reinterred at Hollywood Forever. Speaking on behalf of the cemetery, Nicole Berman noted that Minnelli not only wanted her mother close by, but also wanted her to be buried close to her children, as plots were purchased for Minnelli and her siblings (Associated Press, 2017). Fittingly, Judy Garland, who is best known for portraying Dorothy in *The Wizard of Oz*, joins the film's director Victor Fleming and the dog who played Toto in the film at Hollywood Forever.

Garland was also a favorite icon in the gay community, and her interment at Hollywood Forever creates another stop for LGBTQ cemetery tourists. Historian Martin Duberman (1994) writes that on June 28, 1969, the day of Garland's funeral, "twenty thousand people had waited up to four hours in the blistering heat to view her body at Frank E. Campbell's funeral home on Madison Avenue and Eightyfirst Street" (p. 235), reminiscent of the thousands who lined the streets outside Campbell's decades before to see Rudolph Valentino's body before it was transported by train to Los Angeles. Duberman notes that transgender activist Sylvia Rivera reflected melodramatically on Garland's death, crying that "the greatest singer, the greatest actress of my childhood is no more. Never again 'Over the Rainbow,' no one left to look up to" (p. 236). Rivera's grief ultimately did not keep her from going out that night, where she made history as part of the Stonewall uprising.

While it may never have the cultural capital of Forest Lawn or Holy Cross, the events hosted by Hollywood Forever create a unique sense of place for tourists, visitors, and fans. How visitors develop relationships with the space of the cemetery changes as their experiences change—longtime celebrity gravers who have toured, strolled, photographed, commemorated, and celebrated at the cemetery now mourn the loss of the intimate sense of belonging once experienced there. Yet like a forgotten classic film star cast in a new role past her prime, Hollywood Forever is gaining new fans and admirers eager to learn its history and appreciate its beauty anew.

References

Associated Press. (2017, January 30). Judy Garland's remains moved from New York to L.A. at wishes of Liza Minnelli, family. *Los Angeles Times*. Retrieved from www.latimes.com/local/lanow/la-me-judy-garland-move-20170130-story.html

Deulund, T. (2014, January 21). Meet the man who curates the crazy cool events at Hollywood Forever Cemetery. *Los Angeles Magazine*. Retrieved from www.lamag.com/culturefiles/meet-the-man-who-curates-the-crazy-cool-events-at-hollywood-forever-cemetery/

Duberman, M. (1994). *Stonewall*. New York, NY: Plume Books.

Gottdiener, M. (1996). *The Theming of America: Dreams, visions, and commercial spaces*. Boulder, CO: Westview Press.

Kammen, M. (2010). *Digging up the dead: A History of notable American reburials*. Chicago, IL: University of Chicago Press.

Lee, C. (2007, May 17). Graveyard Shift: For a good time, says L.A.'s hipster hyphenate Gina Gershon, call Hollywood Forever Cemetery. *Los Angeles Times*. Retrieved from http://articles.latimes.com/2007/may/17/news/wk-cover17

Lynch, T. (2000). *Bodies in motion and at rest: On metaphor and mortality*. New York, NY: W. W. Norton & Co.

Mitford, J. (1998). *The American Way of Death Revisited*. Rev. ed. New York: Vintage Books.

Palmer, G. (1993). *Death: The Trip of a Lifetime*. San Francisco: HarperCollins.

Spindler, A. M. (1998, November 15). Getting In. *New York Times Sunday Magazine*. Retrieved from www.nytimes.com/1998/11/15/magazine/getting-in.html

Tabrys, J. (2017, May 22). Chris Cornell's death transcends the typical celebrity death grief process. Uproxx.com. Retrieved from http://uproxx.com/music/chris-cornell-grief-process/

Index

For Product Safety Concerns and Information please contact our EU representative GPSR@taylorandfrancis.com
Taylor & Francis Verlag GmbH, Kaufingerstraße 24, 80331 München, Germany

www.ingramcontent.com/pod-product-compliance
Lightning Source LLC
LaVergne TN
LVHW020651100826
845148LV00012B/2425

* 9 7 8 0 3 6 7 5 2 1 2 1 9 *